D1713362

Advance Prai
Coming Home

"*Coming Home* is a compelling and deeply intimate story of spiritual birth. It takes us through life's inevitable hard truths and diverse initiations—fated rites of passage—that test the caliber of our consciousness through spirit and matter. Chiron describes the impossible agony of his physical condition, the dead ends of his journey, and what it took (and still takes) to be there to tell the story. This book is a celebration of spirit and life through the density of physical incarnation, and for that it may serve to guide many."

—**Maurice Fernandez**, evolutionary astrologer, author of
Astrology and the Evolution of Consciousness,
www.mauricefernandez.com

"Our profound human journey of coming home to our true nature, so uniquely described by Chiron Yeng's brilliant healing story, has touched my heart forever. Born a highly sensitive person myself, I'm sure that those with the good fortune to dive into Chiron's unapologetic questions, brutal honesty, and clear insights will enter an infinite source of exploring new ways of seeing, feeling, living, and being. Everyone's enlightenment journey is indeed uniquely different, and *Coming Home* is helping us develop our collective, enlightened qualities, bringing forth the many shifts in healing perspectives our world needs right now, for us to live together in peace, love, joy, and inner harmony."

—**Hira Hosèn**, TantraOfTheHeart.com

"*Coming Home* by Chiron Yeng is filled with healing insights through many personal and vulnerable real-life experiences. More than eve the world today could use the inspiration of empowered vulnerability where people such as Chiron have found their greatest strength within their greatest weakness. I found it very meaningful reading the book from a first-person perspective and witnessing the heroic healing journey as a lifelong one, from early childhood through the steps of human-consciousness maturation. Knowing firsthand the struggle that Chiron has gone through by healing from his auto-immune health condition, I deeply honor the dedication to the resolution of human suffering that he shares in the book—and in his life—through the application of ancestral-wisdom traditions from across the world."

—**Roman Hanis**, co-founder of Paititi Institute, director of the Center for Indigenous Medicine, traditional Ando-Amazonian and Chinese medicine man

"*Coming Home* is a vibrant journey from despair to miraculous healing. Chiron, a true warrior, confronts his deepest shadows and emerges victorious. The book provides a deep appreciation for life's simplicity and reveals the magic of connecting with our roots. Through the key theme of forgiveness, and a brave choice to relinquish victimhood, the narrative unfolds beautifully, illustrating the power of vulnerability, family reconciliation, and the Universal truth acceptance is a gateway to love and profound healing. The book inspiring testament to the extraordinary magic within the ordinary journey of self-discovery. *Coming Home* is a vibrant, healing experience—a road map from despair to the fullness of our essence."

Dr. Kulvi Kaur, epigenetic scientist, yogi, and TEDx speaker of "Be the Change You Wish to See In Your Cells"

"Chiron's healing journey is a true testament to the world that only by accepting who we really are, can we be healed inside out. This book provides a comprehensive explanation of spiritual healing, the aim being to inform, encourage, and enlighten the reader. In easily understandable terms, it describes the background of healing, how to tap into the universal energy, and how to discover oneself. The home that Chiron comes to echoes more than a physical home, it is the spaciousness of our inner consciousness that we all long to go back to. As Chiron said, he is not healing you, but rather you are the one healing yourself. All you need to do is just embark on the journey."

—**Vancelee Teng,** creative director, curator, and author of *Journeys Around My Hotel Rooms*

Coming Home

Coming Home

A MEMOIR

How I Courageously Loved Myself Into a Life of Wonder *and* Ordinary Magic

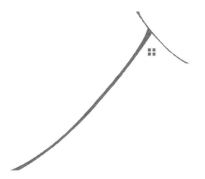

CHIRON YENG

KUALA LUMPUR

Coming Home

Edited by Shannon Littrell
Cover art and illustration by MooiYean Tung
Book design and layout by Jodi McPhee

www.ChironYeng.com

*For all the wounded souls seeking to come home
to the brilliance of your true nature.
This one is for you.*

"Know Thyself, Love Thyself, Heal-thy Self."

—Chiron Yeng

Contents

Is This Book for You?

Not sure if courageously loving yourself and your chronic disease has the potential to change everything? Here are some burning doubts that many have before they begin their hero's journey to come home toward their healing and actualization of their greatest human potential.

1. WHAT IF I DON'T BELIEVE IN SELF-LOVE?

Yes, I too once had a similar experience. I often hear people using the term "self-love," but it is often vague and misunderstood. Self-love is about recognizing that love already exists within you, and it takes a hero's journey for this realization to become self-evident. As shared in *Coming Home*, it reflects both a personal and universal spiritual journey of rediscovering yourself as love. It involves understanding that you are already whole and complete just as you are. Miraculous healing and actualizing your heart's greatest desires naturally arise from this self-rediscovery. Self-love is not a matter of belief. However, allowing yourself the opportunity to believe in it until you find concrete, direct experiences in your life can help you begin your very own hero's journey.

2. WHAT IF MY PARENTS AND DOCTORS DISAPPROVE OF ME SEEKING ADVICE FROM SOURCES THAT ARE NOT SCIENTIFI- CALLY CREDIBLE?

I was in a position where my parents, doctors, spiritual teachers, and holistic healers were making choices and decisions for me. Despite coming from intentions of love, the act of pressuring me to make choices and decisions according to their worldview had made me disconnected from my gut instinct and intuition even further. These fear-based interactions had created chronic diseases and disharmony in my body, mind, and spirit, rather than providing healing. *Coming Home* reflects my personal spiritual and healing journey and does not in any way intend to give any form of medical advice to anyone. However, the key teachings in these books can reveal insights as to why you are stuck in your chronic disease and how you can potentially transform it.

3. WHAT IF I TRIED IT ALL AND I AM STILL FEELING STUCK BY MY CHRONIC DISEASE? HOW CAN THIS BOOK HELP?

I've been there myself, and I know how it feels to experience hopelessness, despair, and anguish. But even in the darkest moments, there is a glimmer of light. All chronic disease is a divine message from the subconscious and an important clue on how we can return to wholeness and remember our true nature. If you find yourself in this place, congratulations—you may be closer to finding the light than you realize. I believe that whatever you're currently doing to heal your chronic disease is already making a difference, and you're just missing one crucial ingredient: learning to love yourself. *Coming Home* tells the story of how I took years to finally understand that self-love is the missing piece to healing. I'm thrilled to be able to save you time, energy, and misery by sharing this wisdom with you.

4. WHAT IF I DON'T CONSIDER MYSELF TO BE A SPIRITUAL PERSON?

You don't need to be a "spiritual" person to start reading this book. In fact, it is a perfect starting point if you are new to spirituality. Having a growth mindset and a beginner's mind is important for reading this book. *Coming Home* is written with an intention of helping you to open your mind and heart to discover new insights and possibilities in your life. If you don't actively seek to expand your perspective, you are limiting yourself from the greater potential and opportunities that your life offers. While religious aspects are mentioned to convey the intended spiritual wisdom in this book, I am not imposing any religiosity or dogma. I am simply discussing secular teachings that you can apply to your lives for your very own personal transformation.

YOU DON'T HAVE TO WALK THIS JOURNEY ALONE.

You don't have to stay stuck in your chronic disease forever. I empower highly sensitive individuals like you to transform self-limiting beliefs and self-sabotaging behaviors, helping you remember your power within to thrive with radiant health and unconditional happiness.

To further support your journey, I'd like to invite you to join a community to receive biweekly newsletters about an opportunity to join an online group healing session. This experience will help you to process difficult emotions that are getting in the way of your healing and empower you to courageously live from your heart.

Join the community here at **www.ChironYeng.com** to experience healing with me.

Foreword

This book provides a mechanism and path to unlock our innate capacities for happiness, success, health, contentment, intuition, unconditional love, beauty, inner peace, and creative flow. These states are within all of us. Yet no one is immune to the trials we all face as human beings. At one time or another we experience grief and loss, trauma and anxiety, overwhelm and burnout, heartache and failure. Sometimes painful experiences are piercing and quick, such as the ripping of a Band-Aid from the skin to avert prolonged agony, while other painful experiences can be relentless and seem to have no end in sight. The latter have been termed, "the dark night of the soul." This book is a lighthouse for you. It is Chiron Yeng's courageous journey through the dark night of *his* soul to awaken and discover his most authentic and empowered self.

As a holistically trained chiropractor, acupuncturist, and developer of The LifeLine Technique®, I can appreciate and value the desire to move quickly through and overcome the pain and stress of life. However, if you're hungry to discern deeper meaning and purpose, and reason and resilience, from situations that don't seem to make sense, Chiron Yeng's story and revelations will help you to discover the most amazing gifts in strange wrapping paper that the pain of life holds.

It has been said that in the moment of complete darkness is the beginning of light. We know from history that unless we're challenged, human nature has a fear-based tendency to settle for the status quo. The consequence is the painful energy in motion stays in motion. That is until it's met by another force. That force is the courage to love your ordinary self.

In this very intimate book, *Coming Home*, Chiron shares timeless wisdom and specific details and steps he took to create real change. Chiron offers a pathway to the freedom that we all long for but find difficult to attain. It may sound counterintuitive to become something by "loving your ordinary self"; however, he certifies through his personal experience that the courage to be your most authentic self is the surest path to inner peace and fulfillment.

I encourage you to read this book with a fresh perspective... as a student. Give yourself permission to explore the pain and stress in your life with honesty, compassion, and curiosity. The first step toward personal transformation through self-healing is acknowledging the need for change. As difficult and painful of a process as that can be, it is important to understand and appreciate that the inner journey is a process. It will require patience, compassion, dedication, and commitment.

I'd like to propose a unique perspective as you dive into

Chiron's story. What we know is this: *What isn't a choice or an action is a reaction.* In a state of reaction, we lack rational thinking, strategic planning, compassion, empathy, and creativity. When in a reactive state, the beliefs of the subconscious mind go on autopilot and take over for the way we perceive ourselves and the world—and even more, act as a magnetic attractor field, bringing forward further circumstances that match the frequency of our limiting and negative beliefs. We do not perceive truth in life; rather, we perceive what we believe.

Beliefs are learned, and not everything that we learn is true—or what may have been true or relevant at one point in time may not be relevant in today's world. Questioning your beliefs and the status quo is necessary to create a portal for evolutionary change. If left unquestioned, the reactive energy and emotions they reflect become a revolution versus an evolution.

Within your heart lies a truth that love is the only answer to fear. What does your heart of love choose to feel? What does your heart of love choose to create? My hope in writing this foreword is to empower you with the knowing that you have the ability to positively change the trajectory of your life. Choose love.

We cannot erase our ugly history, nor would it be beneficial to do so. Our mission and our vision is to awaken the next greatest version of ourselves. It's important to remember, the strongest trees live in the strongest winds. You are here to shine your beautiful, worthy, and very capable light. Your life has purpose, and life's suffering has meaning. The emergence of a worldwide conscious movement of positive focus and evolutionary change for humankind to be kind humans has begun.

Chiron Yeng is a dear friend, brilliant teacher, and beacon of light in our world. I'm so honored for the opportunity to write the foreword of this conscious awakening book. Even further, I'm grateful that Chiron has created a platform for critical and conscious dialogue based upon his own life's journey, travels, and passion to make a positive impact in the world. May his vision of being ordinarily himself inspire you to take an empathic look at the mindset of the dark night of your own soul, so you can learn, heal, and shine as the most authentic and integrity-based expression of love and light you are intended and destined to be.

As the cultural anthropologist Margaret Mead is noted as saying, "A small group of thoughtful people could change the world. Indeed, it's the only thing that ever has." In this beautifully written and compelling book, the inner-connective patterns of being are woven together to reveal the courage to love your ordinary self.

Keep shining bright!

With Infinite Love & Gratitude,

—Dr. Darren Weissman

Best-selling author of *The Power of Infinite Love & Gratitude* and developer of The LifeLine Technique®

Dark Night of the Soul

"How is it possible that a being with such sensitive jewels as the eyes, such enchanted musical instruments at the ears, and such a fabulous arabesque of nerves as the brain can experience itself as anything less than a god? How is it conceivable that this incarnation of all eternity can be bored with being?"

—Alan Watts, *The Book: On the Taboo Against Knowing Who You Are*

Being alive has to be the most mysterious enigma that we can possibly decipher.

Who am I?

Why am I here?

What am I supposed to do and be while I'm alive?

These are existential questions that initiate our intention to study our life's story. At some point in our lives, we become truth seekers who are intrigued about how we can live the most meaningful life we can. Despite not having concrete answers, we find quite a bit of satisfaction in pursuing these endless possibilities.

As a highly sensitive child, my imagination was wild and vivid, and I attempted to make sense of the world I lived in. That deep desire to comprehend life eventually turned me into a truth seeker, which subsequently led me on a personal healing quest. While walking this path, I came to learn that there are no coincidences. There exists a common narrative that speaks about the human spiritual path, where we must go through various forms of crises that are designed to help us remember our true nature.

And my own life story played out in just such a manner.

When I was a child, I developed an autoimmune skin condition. This mysterious illness plagued me from childhood on and continued throughout my teens—all the way to adulthood. The available known solutions to resolve this matter were futile. Life threw a monkey wrench into my plans, and the Universe seemed to have its own idea of how my life was supposed to turn out. This health crisis forced my family and me into a deeper inquiry.

What had we done wrong?

In retrospect, my physical illness reflected a greater dysfunction on the mental, emotional, societal, environmental, and spiritual levels. The illness was a perfect mirror for how disconnected my family and I were from our true natures and how misaligned we were about how life was fundamentally supposed to work.

Consequently, a crisis (which is defined as "a change that must happen, for better or for worse") had to happen to me. It was a course correction from the Universe that was meant to serve me rather than going against me by showing me the way back home to my true nature. The health crisis became an invitation that I wasn't able to refuse, and an initiation into the deeper mysteries of who I was meant to be.

As depicted in Michelangelo's painting *The Creation of Adam*, my choice was to reach out to the finger of God just like Adam did, to actualize my divine nature in physical form.

Nevertheless, it wasn't always smooth sailing. I stubbornly resisted the invitation for the longest time, just like Adam, who looked apathetic in the painting.

The painting reflected the idea that God was more persistent in our actualization process than Adam was. Their fingers never touched, and from God's facial expression, it appeared that He was trying harder than Adam, just like the Universe was persistent in knocking on my door, asking me to self-actualize.

Sooner or later, I learned from experience that resisting the invitation perpetuated more pain and suffering than accepting the call to venture into the unknown.

After being beaten up many times by my own pride and ignorance, I surrendered willingly to the journey, posing a persistent question within my fiery heart: *What is the true purpose of pain and suffering in the human experience?*

I was determined to get to the bottom of this issue. I needed to know the truth of the matter. Intuitively, I knew that there was a greater meaning to my health crisis. Being free from health symptoms simply wasn't good enough for me. Hence, I was constantly questioning the deeper meaning of pain and suffering while hoping for the salvation to land on my feet.

I eventually discovered that there was a phrase to describe this unwelcome invitation and initiation: *the dark night of the soul.* Human suffering wasn't exclusive to me alone. Through conversations with strangers from all walks of life, speaking to friends who had intertwined their fates with me in my journey, and learning from spiritual teachers who were supposed to have it all together, I discovered that we were all in the same boat.

Everyone was going through something, everybody had something to heal, and every soul was looking for a way back home to their true nature.

We were all going through a *dark night of the soul.*

HEALING IS A SELF-ACTUALIZATION JOURNEY

We are all chosen and initiated by life in specific ways.

We have to go through certain lessons to uncover hidden gems and remember our higher purpose.

We are all climbing our very own mountain of trauma to remember and reclaim our rightful place in this universe, solely to remember who we are and why we're here.

And within that remembrance lies our unique creative potential.

But exactly what is this unique creative potential? The best way to put it is in the word *entelechy*, which means "the fullest realized essence of a thing." More than a thing, it is the fully realized essence of a living being. It is our spirit, the love and innate intelligence of the Universe manifesting in our bodily form.

For instance, a butterfly is the entelechy of a caterpillar, while a beautiful lotus flower is the entelechy of a lotus seed. I dare not say that I know the entelechy of a human, but I believe that the entelechy of *being* human is to become enlightened individuals who both honor our authentic self-expression and are able to cultivate harmonious relationships with others and with life. This endeavor to reconcile the self, others, and life is a challenging and arduous journey that only a few in history have successfully accomplished.

Everyone's enlightenment journey is uniquely different. But what I knew for myself when embarking on this journey is that I needed to develop the qualities of *a strong back, a soft front, and a wild heart,* which corresponded to the qualities of wisdom, compassion, and courage, respectively. My vision for myself was that by completing this journey, I would have the possibility to evolve from *Homo sapiens* to *Homo luminous*, a mythic and symbolic expression of a human being who embodies the quintessential expression of love.

I had fortunate encounters with rare individuals who have chosen their very own journey of actualizing their entelechy. They shared a common innate desire between them—to be in servitude of life through love. They embodied qualities of a strong back, a soft front, and a wild heart; and through their backstories, I came to know that these qualities were cultivated by enduring experiences of human pain and suffering, willingly and courageously. It was never about moving away from human pain and suffering, nor was it about moving against them. Rather, it was always about moving toward them and through them gracefully.

Similarly, trials and tribulations seemed to be the Universe's way of invoking such intelligence within me. Pain and suffering became the very catalyst and portal that opened me up to the possibility of Divine Grace. Through these life crises, I was ultimately learning to become who I ordinarily and authentically was all along. What I was seeking was none other than coming home to who I was from the inside, rather than attaining something outside of myself.

There were many times when I thought my life was doomed and that I was destined to be miserable. I thought there was no way out and that I was stuck in a simulation of cause and effect that continued to reproduce itself like the Ouroboros serpent eating its own tail to create an infinite loop. I lamented my life situation many times and complained over and over that the human condition was unfair to begin with. I felt like a child throwing a tantrum at the Universe just because things weren't going in my favor.

Could I blame myself?

I experienced the world as a cold and disconnected place where there was little to no reference at all to living ordinarily and authentically, or any support for what it meant to be the best version of one's entelechy. I saw that many of my friends and those who were on a similar journey were as lost as I was. We felt that we were inherently not enough, that others were not enough, and that the world was not enough.

It didn't matter whom I met in the world. Most of us who subscribed to modern values with little to no exposure to any spiritual practices were burdened by this severe frustration. Not many of us actually had the opportunity to turn within to inquire and began an honest conversation with our inner selves. Looking at the world with such a perspective, we turned ourselves into hungry ghosts. No matter how much we did, we never satiated that eternal hunger for unconditional love and acceptance.

Could I blame the world?

By enduring repetitive cycles of pain and suffering, I realized that the brokenness was neither in the world nor within us, but in the broken lens through which we had chosen to see and experience the world, including ourselves. We were definitely all works in progress.

Hidden behind my healing journey was one of self-actualization. One of the key remedies for healing that I found was to have the courage to be ordinarily me and to radically accept all the imperfect nuances of being human. I realized that without radical self-acceptance, there were no magical methods, supplements, diet/lifestyle/mindset changes, blessings, or energy healings that could help me. My human experience was made and designed for me to get sick, to succumb to pride, and to immerse myself in myriad crises.

But again and again, the Universe continually presented me with a *choice*, just like God in *The Creation of Adam*. The awareness of this choice only came during dire moments when I wanted to give up on my life. It was only when I was down on my knees, beaten up squarely by my own pride and ignorance, and crying tears of surrender, that I could hear the guidance from the Universe.

And in that gentle voice, I always heard the question: "Do you want to write your own story, or do you want your story to be written for you?"

I had learned that despite the seemingly fated circumstances, there was always one last freedom, which was my free will. No one could take my free will away from me, not even God! That sounds liberating, but this was also why God wasn't able to help me—especially in moments when I didn't help myself. I had the last call, and the last opportunity for freedom, to choose how I would experience my circumstances.

I knew what I chose during those moments of crisis. And even today, I'm still choosing that very same thing.

I chose to rise above those trials and tribulations, and like those who have walked the path before me, I chose to be my very own version of *Homo luminous* and be the highest expression of love that I could be.

This is why I find my individual story so intriguing. If a

broken, meek, and feeble person like me can make such a courageous choice, so can *anyone*.

I believe that we are all the inspiring heroes of our own stories as well as sovereign kings and queens in our own lives. As we gain the courage to live our stories fully, our individual universes collide with others', creating a ripple effect of wisdom, compassion, and courage that spreads through the human collective. I see that behind all the brokenness of the world and within our hearts, there are told and untold stories waiting to burst into the rapture of expression.

What are we waiting for?

What are we holding back?

What are we preparing for, if not to be fully alive in this moment right now?

In fact, *now* is the very moment we're waiting for, holding back, and preparing for. The very essence and intelligence of the Universe cannot resist coming alive through each and every one of us. One person's inspiring story is like a flame to all the unenlightened candles. When we have the courage to love and be ordinarily who we are, to live our lives and share our stories, we contribute to the greater whole without doing anything in particular. When we love and become who we ordinarily are, we give others the unspoken permission to do the same.

All it takes is a tiny spark to light up the whole world.

So, what will you choose?

To be authors of our own lives is to be authorities in our own lives—that is, perhaps, the one and only purpose of life. We are here to take our rightful place in this universe, not by resisting or breaking through any trials and tribulations—but by embracing all of them as circumstances that are happening not *to* us, but *for* us. Only by doing so will our true essence and the brilliant intelligence within us have the chance to reveal itself.

Contrary to common human assumptions, purpose is not meant to be done, found, or made. Instead, the purpose of life is to be *revealed*. And it can only be revealed by living our lives fully and coming home to who we truly are, because we are the very purpose that we're looking for.

And the question remains: *Who are we?*

This book is an intimate and honest conversation starter that we can have with ourselves. I invite you to begin the journey to *know thyself* to *love thyself*—and eventually *heal thyself*.

The healing/self-actualization journey is a lonesome one, and no one can walk it for us. However, we can certainly walk our unique paths together.

So, let us step into the journey of loving and becoming who we ordinarily are, and along the way, let us create that beautiful world that we know is possible.

How to Read This Book

I wrote this book from the perspective of a *highly sensitive person*, but I didn't know that I was one myself until I found psychologist and author Elaine Aron's research and successfully ticked all of the boxes in her self-test quiz during the early years of my healing journey. I discovered that this type of person processes life experiences deeply, has a keen awareness of subtle nuances and hidden emotions, and has the ability to intuitively understand complex relationship dynamics. This also means constantly processing sensory information on the nervous system that leads toward constant emotional distress, "analysis paralysis," sensory overload, and feeling overwhelmed.

As a highly sensitive person, I have written this book descriptively and metaphorically to bring you into my inner world, which can lead to multiple interpretations. Therefore,

I suggest that you start reading this book with a beginner's mind and from the standpoint of how you might feel if you were in my shoes. After that, I welcome you to create meaning that is relevant to you and your own life.

Reading this book is a journey from the head to the heart, and finally, into an embodiment of the self. I recommend that you read it by yourself first before you start sharing your reflections with anyone else. When you allow your reflections to sit within you long enough, deeper connections and deeper insights will surface.

Throughout these pages, I invite you to use this opportunity to contemplate your own life. During this contemplation, pay attention to any "aha" moments, and notice the visceral sensations in your body. After all, the energy that your body receives doesn't lie! Allow what may come at first on the intellectual level to sink into an emotional experience, and all the way into a visceral sensation in your body. My intention is for you to experience my *journey* as if it were your own, and as a result, you will experience my *healing* as if it were your own as well.

You will find that I explore the depths of my subconscious, where most of the deep physical and emotional wounds of my humanity are revealed and exposed in this book. Since our conscious minds are interconnected, there will be parts of my story that will trigger your own personal emotional wounds. If there are moments that are triggering for you, take deep breaths; take full responsibility for your physical, mental, and emotional well-being by deeply listening to your body; and regulate your nervous system accordingly, the best way you know how.

At the same time, I encourage you to move *through* any discomfort rather than moving *away* from it. So, try to remember two keywords as you're reading this book: *vulnerability* and *safety*. The presence of these two qualities is when healing occurs! In that respect, please read this book slowly and intentionally. Read it when you're not distracted and with *loving awareness*. Pause, taking breaks and spaces in between the chapters, so that you can fully take in what is being shared.

The truth of the wisdom written here is not mine alone, but represents contributions from many seen and unseen sentient beings who have helped shape me into who I am today. I offer gratitude to them for delivering this timeless and universal wisdom, as they show us all a path where we can remember our entelechy, especially in times of darkness. By writing down my stories, I hope to memorialize the insight and wisdom that transcends space and time and contribute to the growth and evolution of our human consciousness.

The wisdom that I share in this book is not something that can be found through any form of external education, but rather, through an inner education that allows you to know who you are, inside and out. Thus, I invite you to make this timeless wisdom your own. Keep a notebook beside you, and write down any phrases that catch your attention. What you want to do with these phrases is to return to them in the future and allow new perspectives to evolve from them.

It doesn't matter when, where, how, or why you're reading this book—I believe there is a deeper reason that only the Universe knows. This gives me the courage to share my stories, because I know that whoever is attracted to this book must have things they need to read about and understand from my own healing and self-actualization journey. Remember, we are reflections—mirrors—of each other! Therefore, I encourage you to set an intention before diving into these pages. And if you're reading this book for the second time or more, set a different intention and see what new insights and perspectives you might discover.

This book is divided into four parts, plus an epilogue and an afterword, with each part representing a key developmental stage in my unique conditioning and how I transformed the limitations of that conditioning into the potential of my entelechy. These key development stages are universal to all but unique to each individual. Using this book as a reflection, and studying these key developmental stages for yourself can help you understand your unique past, which will help you liberate your present and create the new future you desire.

PART ONE: INCARNATION is where I discuss my birth story and explore the existential meaning of what it means to be human. Birth marks the beginning of our life, and most of the time we have little to no memories of it. Nevertheless, the body keeps score, and no memories are lost—only forgotten. When we can understand the environment we're born into, we can understand the hard wiring of our limiting beliefs, behaviors, and habits that are holding us back from our entelechy.

PART TWO: CONDITIONING reflects my unique childhood conditioning and how I recovered the lost essence of my authentic self-expression. Childhood is a time when we are the truest to who we are, as well as a time when our innocence is also lost. When our authentic self-expression is not honored, supported, and appreciated, we tend to repress this trait out of protection, fearing that we may not be loved for who we are. Hence, for most of us, we end up becoming someone we're not, adopting a false persona that conforms to societal expectations. However, the opportunity here is to consciously recover this innocence, as well as our authentic self-expression. When we can do so, we tap into both our inner power and our self-healing potential.

PART THREE: CONNECTION represents my adolescent and young adult years and how I made sense of the concepts of love, leadership, and relationships. Here, I explore how I attempted to create a harmonious sense of belonging with others in a world that is built on false ideas of love, leadership, and relationships. This is important to unpack, because as much as we would like a formula for true love and authentic connection, there is none other than being created by our own vision and our ever-growing understanding of it.

PART FOUR: TRANSFORMATION takes a deep dive into the transformational journey of my physical health. Behind my healing journey is a self-actualization journey of becoming a spiritual and peaceful warrior who has a strong back, a soft front, and a wild heart in the world. This is an initiation, because through the unique experience of my disease, it opened me up to a whole new understanding of why it had to show up in my life in the first place.

Finally, in the epilogue and afterword, I wrap up the book by sharing how I courageously loved myself into a life of wonder and ordinary magic, and finally led myself to come home to my true nature.

Throughout these pages, you will notice that I interchangeably use uppercase *U* and lowercase *u* to describe the "universe." The uppercase *Universe* is a personification of the almighty presence that comes in many names in different spiritual studies and traditions such as Atman, Higher Self, Love, Dao, Source, Great Spirit, Super Conscious Mind. Otherwise, it is most commonly known as God. It's capitalized because I acknowledge this presence as a living and intelligent sentient yet formless being whom I respect, humbly bow down to, and frequently have conversations with. Hence, for clarity purposes, the uppercase Universe represents both divine forces of life that are outside of me and the God consciousness within me. In contrast, the lowercase *universe* represents the actual space of the living or the cosmos, the mundane activities of our human life, or our subjective experiences of life.

Also, please note that in this book, I explore my personal journey with spirituality, which is inspired by different religious traditions and philosophical ideas from around the world. In particular, Buddhism, Taoism, evolutionary astrology, Greek mythology, New Age spirituality, and Native American shamanism have informed my worldview. Despite mentioning the religious aspects to convey the intended spiritual wisdom in this book, I'm not pushing any religiosity or dogma onto you, my readers, but merely discussing secular teachings that you can implement into your lives.

With deep prayers, I hope that this book resonates with those of you who are calling out for the Universe's grace and love the most.

Let us all remember the preciousness of living existence and embrace the totality of being fully alive. Take a journey with me as you begin to embark on your own healing journey and come home to your true nature. The homecoming journey isn't always easy; in fact, it invites more challenges along the way. Regardless, it's still a path worth embarking on, and possibly the most self-fulfilling path available for all of us.

May my work serve as a guidepost and source of inspiration and encouragement for you as you sail through the waves of life with courage and deeper understanding. I offer this work humbly, in infinite love and gratitude.

May there be love, light, and truth shining your path forward.

You are enough. Your ordinariness is extraordinary.

PART ONE

Incarnation:
The Courage to Be Here

"Life does not feed life. Life is on the receiving end of life. Always. No, it is death that feeds life. It is the end of life that gives life a chance. Human beings aren't born. Human beings are made."

—Stephen Jenkinson, "The Meaning of Death"

CHAPTER ONE

Not All Who Wander
Are Lost

I was walking alone along the sandy beaches of Encinitas, California—a coastal community outside of San Diego—during the summer of 2015. After years of traveling, I was already used to going solo. I simply took myself wherever my heart felt like roaming. Being lost in a place where no one knew who I was felt like the most liberating experience my heart could yearn for. I had grown accustomed to having solitude as my trusted companion.

It was close to dusk, and the twilight from the far end of the horizon made the sea look like it was on fire. My feet left crimson footprints on the sand, which would soon be washed away by the waves of the ocean. The ebbs and flow of nature (whom I like to refer to as "her") were so evident, and everything was subject to impermanence. Being in this setting made me feel like I was in a trance. I felt incredibly peaceful, like I was part of nature's dance.

What appeared eventually disappeared.

My peace was interrupted by an angst-like feeling of discontentment. It started out as harmless awareness about the chronic pain in my body. However, the more I focused on it, the more it turned into a feeling of scarcity and unworthiness.

I felt like I had chosen the short end of the stick and fate had dealt me a bad hand. It didn't take long for self-pity to emerge, and before I realized it, I started seeing the world around me from the standpoint of a victim. In a split second, I was triggered, and I began to experience an emotional downward spiral.

My thoughts started to erupt with complaints. My mind tried to find evidence for why things in life never went the way they were supposed to. I wondered where everything had gone wrong for me.

Why is this happening to me?

I found that I never seemed to be able to enjoy what was in front of me. There was a sense of urgency that I had to get on to the next thing, to the next, and to the next—but hopefully one day I would finally get it right, successfully reclaim my life, and feel like it was under my control.

Watching the vastness of the sea, I felt spacious, yet completely isolated from the world. A moment ago, I had been mesmerized by the beauty of nature, yet now, this beauty was tainted by the reminder of the human ugliness that committed atrocities upon her. I felt the need to do something about it, but I also felt helpless to make any difference.

These problems were way beyond me, anyway.

My hands were already full of my own problems.

This wasn't my first experience observing the insanity of my own mind. In fact, I'd been watching it for years. The first time I attempted meditation, my mind went wild. Thoughts were flying in all directions, and it felt like water was pounding on my head—as if I were sitting under a waterfall. I thought I was the only one feeling that way until I met others who shared that their experiences were exactly like mine, or even worse. Thank God for that feedback; otherwise, I might have thought I was going crazy.

Practicing meditation with a group helped me understand that the human mind skews toward the negative, and our thoughts have an uncanny ability to amplify those negative feelings. Whatever we focus on, grows. My meditation teachers called this "the monkey mind." And I called my mind "the wild monkey mind," which needed to be tamed.

Initially, taming the wild monkey mind felt like a discipline where I would try to have no thoughts at all. But after familiarizing myself with meditation, I discovered that having no thoughts at all wasn't the point. Rather, the point was to allow what needed to come up to surface, and then disappear like the tides of the ocean. Taming wildness had nothing to do with controlling anything, but instead, befriending what was alive in the present moment.

I envied how nature was able to constantly change her shape and form, following a rhythm through the seasons and cycles without being attached to the past. She looked like she was just following through into the next phase effortlessly. Unlike me, who was always trying get to the next thing urgently.

Nature never rushed while she was changing.

And the best part was—when uninterrupted—everything usually evolved right on time, in the way that it was supposed to. Nature had no goals yet always arrived impeccably at where she needed to be. Nature probably didn't have any aspirations, like wanting to save the world or saving herself, and yet, when left alone, she easily healed in her own way. I wished I could be like her.

For me, the human mind was a torturous place to be. I almost wished I could have shared this moment with someone. Then, perhaps, these intrusive thoughts wouldn't have plagued me.

But that wasn't what I was looking for or why I was wandering aimlessly on the beach in the first place. I wasn't seeking any sort of companionship. I wasn't searching for anyone or anything to make me feel better, either. I didn't want any more interventions. I just wanted to melt into nature's beauty and let the waves of the ocean wash away my sense of self-awareness.

Something was amiss within me.

Something needed to be filled.

New traveling experiences, hedonic pleasures, and lovely companions didn't seem to do the trick. They felt temporal, and at the end of the day, I was still stuck within myself. I often described this emptiness within me as "a longing from my heart."

Longing for what, exactly?

Heck, I don't know!

It wasn't a comfortable feeling, and this wasn't the first time I had felt it. But at least I knew that there was something poking from within, seeking my attention. Most people described this as depression or loneliness. Many had bluntly recommended that I engage in more social activities and creative outlets to get things going again.

But I secretly detested this advice. It made me feel worse, and for some reason, I experienced people's concern as insulting lip service, as if it was taboo for me to feel depressed or be alone.

Strangely, I wanted the very opposite of what they thought was good or right for me. I wanted to *feel* these feelings and get to the bottom of them. I was angry most of the time because these painful emotions were below the surface. So I rebelled against people's kindness.

I was rebellious because my authentic feelings were being denied and assaulted. Simultaneously, I had also learned to repress these feelings for fear of rejection. I was afraid that if I shared openly or asked for what I truly needed, then people would find me ridiculous rather than genuinely holding a safe and protective space for me. So I internalized that anger and unintentionally turned it against myself.

I felt that no one seemed to understand why it was important to me that others witness and accept my darker human emotions. So, I withdrew deeper and deeper into my own internal caverns, making sure that no one knew what was happening to me. The loneliness I felt wasn't caused by a lack of human interaction, but by the lack of people's sensitivity to the whole spectrum of my human experience.

I particularly noticed this aching feeling within my heart when I had no choice but to socialize in the presence of a large crowd. This was why I avoided attending birthday parties and networking events, or why I tended not to go to clubs and festivals. The aching only got worse when, by chance, I would be in a group where people were engaging in small talk and exchanging superficial glances as the only agreeable forms of social connection. I found it difficult to trust what was coming out of people's mouths, and I didn't know how to respond authentically without offending anyone.

That made me feel lonely.

During moments when I had to share something about myself, I had to bring up the inconvenient topics of my health condition and my peculiar dietary restrictions. I brought up these issues because most social engagements were done in the presence of food, and I had to awkwardly reject people when they offered it to me. This was another instance when I experienced these aching feelings. A part of me was desperate to be included in social groups, but at the same time, I was afraid of losing myself in front of these people. If I succumbed to people-pleasing, I was the one who ultimately ended up suffering. This aching pain got worse when people were quick to give advice and suggestions on how I could feel better without understanding what was going on in the first place.

That made me feel lonely.

There were also moments when I felt that my existence was completely invalidated, just like other people invalidated their own lives when they allowed their precious attention to get sucked into their phones. Their efforts to express empathy were painful to watch. They were mostly acting out of pity, as if impatiently waiting for me to be done feeling sorry for myself so that they could go back to their own lives. Those were the moments that made me feel as if my suffering was an inconvenience to others. Perhaps what I had to share was too painful for them to bear witness, as it reminded them of their own pain.

And that, too, made me feel lonely.

In rejection of their own pain, they had rejected mine. I believed that the world didn't understand me, and I felt out of place. The "normality" of life didn't seem ordinary, natural, or healthy to me, but many people continued to live superficially, as if that were the only option for them. Everyone was walking on eggshells. They were overly careful to not rock the boat or stir up any triggering feelings in others.

I found that rather displeasing. Chronic loneliness eventually evolved into chronic bitterness and resentment, which made me judgmental as hell. And the worst part of all was that I noticed that I was doing the very same thing that I was judging others for. I felt ashamed of myself. It was like a knee-jerk reaction that I had absolutely no control over.

One example was when people tried to make eye contact with me on an elevator, and I simply averted my eyes. When people asked me, "How are you?" I usually pushed that question away with a monotonous and robotic "I'm good," when, actually, I was not doing well at all. I felt that I was acting in a superficial manner, my body demeanor awkward, and I didn't feel that I was pleasant to be around. Deep down, I just wanted to be done connecting with people so that I wouldn't risk opening my heart and getting hurt again.

When I wasn't able to run away from a conversation, I habitually deflected it by turning the very same question back to the other person. I preferred to listen to the problems of others rather than sharing my own, to avoid feelings of vulnerability and rejection.

The truth was, people never did outright reject me. But the disconnection I felt in their presence made me feel as if they had.

Since I was someone who had delved into my own pain, other people often found me to be an attentive listener, and they seemed to enjoy sharing their painful experiences with me. Many commented that my tone of voice was trustworthy and soothing. For some reason, my voice made them felt safe, as if it were an invitation for them to open up.

But to be completely honest, I was mostly being attentive not out of a concern for others, but out of a self-absorbed need to hide my pain from them. In return, I became the dumping site for many people's emotional garbage. I didn't want to say no to them because that would have made me feel like a hypocrite.

If I judge people for not being present and authentic with my pain, how can I not be present for the pain of others?

Fearing my very own judgment, I got stuck in a vicious, self-destructive habit of carrying the pain of others and the world.

What kept my sanity intact was nature. There were no expectations from her. There was no judgment. There was no fixing me or helping me. Nature was a perfect mirror and a sanctuary for me to be just as I was. Hence, rather than sitting in my hotel room watching Netflix or forcing myself to be with other people, walking around aimlessly in nature felt like a better option.

I first learned how to do so when I learned the concept of *sauntering* from reading Henry David Thoreau. Sauntering was one of those words that I had never forgotten. From time to time, this exact word popped up in my mind as if the Universe was calling on me to go out for a walk. As aimless as those walks might have been, they weren't without intention.

Thoreau shared that the secret for successful sauntering was to walk everywhere as if everywhere was home. And nature was home to all, but not a commodity to be owned by others. It was still a strange concept to me that we were able to own lands and put our names on this good earth.

The epitome of sauntering was also aptly described in J.R.R. Tolkien's famous quote from *The Lord of the Rings:* "Not all those who wander are lost." There was a great deal of truth behind those words. In retrospect, perhaps what was amiss within me was this sense of home, which wasn't so much a physical place but a state of being that felt lost and disconnected throughout the years of my overly protected, sanitized, and domesticated upbringing.

Perhaps I had to get lost to reconnect to what was essential to me all along.

Throughout my sauntering experiences, I realized that I had lost something so precious and dear to me—the wildness of my humanity. Perhaps my mind went wild because my heart was overly tamed with self-control. And to tame my wild monkey mind, perhaps I had to first set my wild heart free.

So, with this very intention, I set out to rediscover and reconnect with any wildness that was left within me. Sauntering in the wildness of nature allowed me to confront this wildness within me. It showed me exactly *where* I was and how broken and disconnected I was.

Perhaps this was the very remedy that I needed to heal my body, mind, and spirit.

Perhaps this was the very home my heart was longing for.

Perhaps this was what snapped me out of the trance of believing that there was a set path in life for everyone to follow and propelled me into the unknown.

And I remembered how this all began very clearly.

In September 2011, I achieved a significant milestone: I completed my A levels (subject-based qualifications conferred by educational bodies in the UK), and had managed to secure an enrollment at the Imperial College of London. Through the eyes of a young adult, I felt like I was on top of the world.

However, only two months into my first semester, I began to feel completely empty from within. The common narrative for a high achiever to secure a placement in a prestigious university and then graduating from one had lost its meaning.

This was a time when the intersection of the yearly season transitioned from autumn to winter. Everything seemed depressing and slow moving. This environment made the confusion and bewilderment that had already been brewing within me start to spiral out of control. It was gloomy, dark, and rainy in London, and I found that the weather mimicked the old-fashioned architecture of old England and my very own emotions as well. Buildings spoke of old tales and many untold stories of the mundane, post-industrialized human condition.

As I walked through the streets of South Kensington, while making my way to the Imperial College of London, I noticed that there were efforts of renewal through the reconstruction and repainting of the outer walls of the buildings. In my own world, I wondered if these buildings were conscious at all and if they had their own thoughts. And if they were able to express them, what were their opinions about us humans? They had passed the test of time, and their presence seemed to be eternal. Maybe they had a suggestion or two for me. Despite running against time to catch a quiz, I stopped to contemplate how much of these timeless buildings had experienced humanity. I wondered if, from their perspective, humans had arrived at the pinnacle of our evolution.

Later that morning, I was taking a math quiz. Despite the heavy silence in the room, the four-sided enclosure was debating loudly while staring down at me as I awaited an appropriate judgment from them. Linear time started to deconstruct itself, and my perception of the room collapsed into a wavelike sea of energy. The math equations started to shape-shift, as if they were questioning my very existence and purpose. The discomfort in my gut caught my attention, and I was confronted with a reality check.

I asked myself, *Am I where I'm supposed to be, doing what I'm supposed to be doing, living out what I'm supposed to live out?*

It was the hardest quiz I had to take, because there was no textbook answer. There were no answers to memorize for, and there was no such things as cheat sheets. I felt like I had been suddenly thrown into the deep sea, where waves were made out of chaos and mayhem, and I had to somehow survive it.

It was sink or swim.

But how I swam was the least of my concerns. I knew that if I didn't at least try, I would definitely drown. I was clenching my teeth very hard with frustration and agony in light of those impossible questions. I had never once failed a quiz, and now I was going to break down in the classroom.

How shameful!

Soon I was breaking out in a cold sweat, and my mind progressively went into a state of paralysis. Sensibility and constructs of my perception were progressively falling apart. I was going through my own "blue screen of death," where there was a fatal system error in my consciousness. This might had been my very first episode of psychosis.

Despite that, I knew the answers to the existential questions very well. I always had the answers. The only resistance was admitting that the answers I had were the truth. It was a difficult pill for me to swallow. The answers simply did not match the common narrative that I knew.

Ever since I had first set foot on the Imperial College of London, I knew that the environment definitely didn't feel congruent with my inner peace. I felt as if people were walking robots, and the geometrical buildings of the university cast away any signs of nature's vibrancy. I felt incarcerated and claustrophobic, while my vitality progressively diminished as I continued to live there. My experience of attending monotonous lectures and classes, participating in meaningless student-club activities, and making superficial connections with new peers in the dormitories were lacking something so very crucial.

I felt a sense of wrongness, but I had no words to describe that feeling or why I felt the way I did. I thought that if I wasn't able to describe something out loud or had any actual logical explanation, then maybe it wasn't real. Those feelings continued to give me the perfect excuse to be in denial. This sense of wrongness usually showed up as a disturbance in the background of my senses, like a splinter poking at me. It was subtle, prickly, and flirtatious, yet very much alive, as if there was an important point to be made.

Sitting in the hot seat of the classroom, my very existence was being challenged.

Is this the pinnacle of my life?

For a moment, I had a glimpse of the future, of what would happen if I stayed to finish the math quiz. My life was playing out right in front of my eyes, and it felt like déjà vu. I had been here before. I had made a choice to conform to this common narrative in the past.

Is this another opportunity for me to make the choice to walk the road less traveled?

Next, I suddenly recalled the position of Neo when he was presented with the blue pill or red pill in the *Matrix* movie.

How is it possible that fictional movies are able to match my current real-life experiences?

I assumed that I must be going crazy.

While experiencing a crack in my psyche and noticing the obvious disharmony between my heart and my mind, I decided to take the red pill.

I had the most brilliant idea—to drop out of my hard-earned placement in this prestigious university, and go on an enigmatic and exciting adventure to seek out life-changing truths. I was enveloped with fear and anxiety, which soon turned into an adrenaline rush similar to the moment when a roller coaster reaches its peak, soon to be free-falling. When the fall came, all my fear and anxiety disappeared. My muscles, which were weak and feeble, and my spirit, which was dull and sullen, suddenly transformed into a vibrancy that I had had never experienced before.

For a moment, I tasted the zest of life. I felt more empowered than ever. My muscles were engaged and ready to run toward a destiny that I couldn't entirely envision. What I had experienced was more invigorating than knowing all the answers to any quizzes I had ever taken.

Deep down, I knew that I had an urgent desire for radical change.

As my prefrontal cortex rebooted, I left the classroom after handing in an empty paper. I was completely disoriented, awaiting a path that was full of uncertainties for the very first time. I walked out of the university, only taking my essentials with me. Instead of taking the underground train, I walked for three hours eastward from South Kensington all the way to Canary Wharf, just for the sake of it. For the very first time, I finally experienced the vibrancy of this metropolitan city, which matched the awakening of my soul.

Ah! This is what it feels like to follow my bliss.

After my time at the Imperial College of London, I ended up reapplying to University College of London (UCL), another prestigious university, in the fall of 2012. This time I took biochemistry as a major, hoping to become a dietitian or a nutritionist someday. The inspiration came from Hippocrates, who said, "Let food be thy medicine, and medicine be thy food." I thought if I had to look after my health, why not be someone who knew all the ins and outs of this discipline? I was also hoping that the negative freshman experience at

Imperial College was a fluke and that I would be able to have a happier experience here.

Alas, I didn't get very far, and my time at UCL ended in the summer of 2013 when lab work in biochemistry completely destroyed my health. Exposed to the chemicals for hours every week, my body reacted with another huge flare-up on my skin, which forced me to put a halt to my education. I knew that I wasn't going to be able to withstand another two years of such stress.

While healing, I decided to take a gap year to do some soul searching and go wherever bliss took me. While following this bliss, I found many philosophical and spiritual books, and also took up the art of dance. In addition to spending hours seeking out answers in newly discovered spiritual books, I was obsessively spending time in dance studios.

I took every opportunity to attend advanced dance classes that were actually too difficult for me. But I did not care one bit if I was a beginner or if I was able to catch up with the rest of the students in the class. There was a deep hunger to learn and be proficient, so I spent most of my waking hours practicing my moves. During moments when I wasn't prac-ticing, I would put my headphones on and lose myself in the world of music while imagining dance moves in my mind. I hoped that through hard work and perseverance, I would be able to get somewhere with dance. For the first time in my life, I was committed to doing something that I authentically chose for myself.

There was something about dance and music that was able to paint my dull life bright again. My experiences in those dance classes were both healing and liberating for me because I was able to access the inner emotions that I had blocked out.

I noticed how numb I had been in my day-to-day life, and dance was able to help me *feel* again.

After attending classes for months, I finally saw that dance was more than just glamor and performances; it was deep inner work that allowed me to express my soul. More than an individual pursuit, I was connected to a community of individuals who lived their lives passionately and purposefully. Being around other dancers, I wasn't alone in my need to feel the rapture of being fully alive, and that consistently brought me to tears. I was immersed in an environment where other individuals were also seeking the same liberating experiences, and I realized that maybe I wasn't that weird, after all. Maybe that was why they danced, and why they continued on this path, even though the process was full of blood, sweat, and tears.

The dance classes I attended were an epitome of what Rumi had shared: "Dance, when you're broken open. Dance, if you've torn the bandage off. Dance in the middle of the fighting. Dance in your blood. Dance when you're perfectly free."

Dance was definitely one of those things that lit up my soul, and I had no second thoughts about allowing this passion to consume me. I acknowledged that I had been playing my life too safe, and I was too concerned with trying to get things just right. My mind was obsessed with taking control.

At this same time, I tried to learn and perform some choreography. What happened on the dance floor was a microcosm that reflected my behaviors about the big things I wanted to do in life. By squeezing every ounce of my blood, sweat, and tears into dance, I learned that what mattered wasn't how perfectly I lived, or how well I mastered the choreography, but how I showed up and moved through the mistakes and imperfections of life. Bit by bit, I discovered how to let loose and let go without getting lost in the chaos.

However, the ecstasy of my dance experience didn't last too long, because a humbling moment struck my life when I stayed longer than I should have in London. The heights of my ecstatic experiences immediately plummeted into the depths of catharsis.

When I went away to Sweden for a short trip and returned to London, I was held off at immigration and wasn't allowed to enter. This was expected, as my student visa had become invalid since I had dropped out of the university. So, the officials picked up my baggage and immediately sent me to a detaining room for further questioning. I got stuck in that room all day, with hardly any interaction with the customs officers. With very little explanation, I was given a ticket to take the next flight to my previous destination, which was Sweden.

Like a tsunami, everything unfolded very quickly, and I had to return to my home country of Malaysia. It was jarring news to all of my peers in London, and in an instant, all of them disappeared from my life as I was swept away geographically back to my native home.

Despite the perpetual confusion and bewilderment during my years in London, the downtime I had on the plane helped me understand why life needed to happen in the way it did. To make sense of these experiences, I reasoned with myself that the Universe was preparing me for something bigger than I was able to imagine and dream of. At first glance, it felt like the Universe was intentionally going against me in every single way, but in hindsight, the Universe did me a favor. Hence, I kept my faith alive by believing in a fulfilling future and surrendering all the little details of how that future was going to play out.

And just like that, my chapter in London ended in the spring of 2014, and a new chapter began.

A couple of months after my return to Malaysia, I had a fortunate encounter with an astrologer who pointed me toward Boulder, Colorado, where Buddhist-inspired, nonsectarian Naropa University was located. Without doing any research or thinking it through, I simply took a spontaneous leap of faith and decided to continue my education at Naropa that fall.

When I finally arrived in the land where American dreams are made, I had the confident intuition that I was finally where I needed to be and that I was taking my first step on my true path. I didn't know what to expect, and that was the point. It was my true path because an unknown path was a path that no one had taken or walked before. Even if this path led to disaster, at least I wasn't repeating a previous narrative. And the only way to confirm such a truth was to move forward, one step at a time.

After passing through immigration smoothly and finally getting out of the airport, I saw a uniquely formed cloud that said "入" (rù) in a Chinese character painted at the backdrop of the blue sky. It simply meant "enter" or "welcome," and there I was, finding myself dumbfounded with the way the Universe was communicating with me. This warm welcome from the Universe gave me the confirmation that I was walking in the right direction. My inner feelings were being matched by an outer symbolism.

What an affirmation!

Despite not knowing what was coming next, this phenomenon gave me the confidence to step into my next chapter. It turns out that *believing is seeing, and seeing is also believing.*

■ ■
■ ■

My reminiscing was interrupted when I noticed the crimson sand slowly fading into darkness. In the distance, the boundaries between the sand and the sea started to fade into one. I paused for a moment to peer into the horizon to experience the final glimpse of the sun before it disappeared.

And again, the boundaries between the sky and the sea started to blur, leaving only artificial light to light up the beach. The horizon gradually vanished, and the night engulfed the presence of living nature from my sight, leaving only the sound of the waves crashing into the shore. With such a spectacular performance from nature, I wondered why no one bothered to give it a standing ovation.

Never mind the standing ovation—how many of us actually took the time and space to be bathed by the presence of God in the form of nature, with deep reverence and gratitude?

As I reminded myself to let simple pleasures guide me, I took a deep breath and allowed myself to absorb the experience of this memory while honoring the setting of the sun and the presence of the night all at once. Duality of nature was what made nature inexplicably beautiful.

For a moment, my loneliness subsided, and all that was left was aliveness in the moment.

I was grateful for how far I had come, navigating those turbulent years, just to be here witnessing nature's glory. In that moment, nothing else mattered. The year of going to school in Boulder had really done wonders for my spiritual growth.

I was finally getting somewhere.

After the darkness completely swept away the remaining light, the local neighborhood of Encinitas was my next area to explore. Some homes were fancy and glamorous, while some were quaint and unique. I wasn't interested in big, trendy "5-star Travel Advisor–rated" places. As a visitor, I was more interested in how people were living their lives here in Southern California. I wondered how much of these homes reflected the personalities of their owners and how they experienced life.

Are they struggling with life's questions, as I am?

Or are they glad that they have so much material abundance?

Do they take the time to appreciate how beautiful it is to be living by the beach?

Or do they get lost worrying about petty first-world problems?

It didn't matter to me how they lived their lives, whether it was right or wrong. It didn't matter if someone else's life was better or worse than another's. I just wanted to know if they were living lives where they felt fully alive, and if they were grateful to have a human incarnation. And if they did, I wondered if they had answers as to why I was experiencing so much discontentment.

I didn't know when it started. I didn't know why I grew to become so distrustful of human nature or how I got so angry with the way the world worked. I didn't know how I started doubting my human experiences and started seeing that my incarnation as a human was a big mistake.

But in that moment, there was an aching pain to find out why I felt the way I did. I was certain that there was a higher meaning somewhere out there, waiting for me to discover it. I was hungry and thirsty for such truths, as I believed that they were the only things that could satiate my inner emptiness, expressed as my heart's ache.

I remembered that when I was a child, I frequently looked up into the sky and was mesmerized by the moon and stars. I was an inquisitive child who was also curious about dinosaurs and pondered who was around before them. I was also that annoying child who asked why too many times, and no one really had any answers for me.

My fascination with the cosmos definitely had given me a sense of certainty that mysteries of the cosmos weren't meant to be kept as secrets, but were merely waiting to be discovered by humans.

Interestingly enough, the biggest mystery of all was right in front of me.

And that was me.

CHAPTER TWO

Inspiration from the Cotton-Clad One

While my mind was busy ruminating as I strolled through the quiet streets of Encinitas, I was reminded of a story about a person who walked the face of this earth courageously. He found love, peace, and harmony despite having a dark past of unforgivable sins and unimaginable anguish. He was lost and didn't know what to do with his existential rage. But with that same rage, he forged a path of unshakable resolution to become an enlightened being.

His name was Milarepa, which means "the cotton-clad one." His heroic journey made him one of the great sages who created the foundations for Tibetan Buddhism.

Milarepa experienced a traumatic event when his father died, and subsequently, he was betrayed by his uncle and aunt. Blinded by rage and his personal sense of righteousness, he sought revenge through black magic. He unleashed destruction on the perpetrators, but his actions took not only the lives of his uncle and aunt but also the lives of innocent bystanders.

His sense of satisfaction stemming from his acts of revenge was short-lived, though, and he soon experienced the implications of his horrendous actions. He was swallowed up by a sense of guilt and remorse for betraying humanity. He realized that he couldn't escape the powerful forces of cause and effect, so he went on a journey of transformation to resolve his anguish.

During the journey, Milarepa made a resolution not to commit such atrocious actions again and to seek repentance. Caught in a web of pain, he also received insights about the incessant dualistic nature of human suffering and longed for liberation. He resolved to transcend the cyclical suffering of birth and rebirth.

His journey led him to Marpa, a spiritual teacher, from whom he hoped to receive transmission of *Buddhadharma,* the true teachings of Buddha and enlightenment. At that time, Marpa was a practitioner who traveled back and forth between India and Tibet, teaching Buddhadharma to his students.

Marpa saw that Milarepa was not worthy and ready for the teachings, and instead made him go through futile and difficult trials. But with his unshakable resolve, Milarepa accomplished them without complaining or wavering. Nevertheless, these trials eventually pushed him to hit rock bottom, as they seemed endless.

Milarepa attempted suicide over his deep remorse for his past actions, which showed Marpa that he was ready to receive the teachings. The trials purged Milarepa's rage, self-righteousness, and negative past actions, giving him a clean slate, which allowed Marpa to transmit the Buddhadharma more efficiently.

Finally, Milarepa received an advanced form of dharma called Mahamudra, which led to his training in the caves of Tibet and finding enlightenment. This enlightenment led him to become "the cotton-clad one" because he was seen to be wearing little even during the freezing winter. Both a masterful yogi and a poet, Milarepa became a teacher of dharma and transmitted the teachings through spontaneous songs and poems of realizations called the "The Hundred Thousand Songs of Milarepa." He eventually became a major figure in the history of the Kagyu school of Tibetan Buddhism.

I held Milarepa's story close to my heart. It reminded me that despite all the tragedies and atrocities inflicted upon, and experienced by, humanity, we are never hopeless. Milarepa's story is an intentional and powerful epic that showed me that no one is beyond redemption—all of humanity has the potential to thrive, actualize entelechy, and express the highest expressions of love. All sentient beings have an equal potential to become fully enlightened.

Our past does not dictate who we are; the choices we make shape our character and the future of humanity. During those times when I endured hopelessness and despair myself, Milarepa's story shone like the only star in the vast darkness of my universe. It was the glimmer of hope that reminded me that someday I would be able to understand the mystery of who I am; reclaim my wildness; and know what bliss, inner peace, and radical acceptance is all about.

The truth was, I was afraid to be here, to exist, to be alive on this earth. Everything felt overly complicated, and I didn't understand the normality of things. One of the most bizarre things about the world was the amount of money invested in weapons of mass destruction and war over solving issues such as world hunger, equal accessibility to education and health care for all, and the impending doom of climate change.

I was both scared and outraged that our predecessors had left us a barren earth, and now it was up to us to do something for future generations. And with that, came fearful neuroses:

I'm afraid that I won't turn out to be the son I'm expected to be.

I'm afraid to fail my future children and the generations to come.

I'm afraid that I have let down the people whose trust and love I yearn for.

I'm afraid that I'm powerless and helpless to do anything about the world's crises.

I'm afraid to make things worse than they already are.

I'm afraid that I have become a lost cause.

I'm afraid that if I show my true self, I'll be rejected.

I'm afraid to be me because of all the brokenness inside me.

I'm afraid that I don't have a choice to be me.

I'm afraid that if I give in to surrender, that is the end of me.

I'm afraid to be authentic, as that shows vulnerability, so I pretend to be something else.

I'm afraid that I will perpetuate the wheel of spiritual undoing and get lost in the world's confused way of living.

I'm afraid that I have no place in this world, no home to belong to, no sanctuary to feel safe in.

I'm afraid that there's no way out, and all the spiritual teachings are just glitters of gold dust that lack real substantial and practicality.

I'm afraid that being human means eventually destroying what is around me because of my conditioned, selfish tendencies.

Naming these fears stirred an urgency within me, and I noticed that the pace of my sauntering had quickened. I felt the need to do something about these concerns immediately.

I had to fix them.

It was up to me.

I had to be the savior.

I felt unworthy to be alive, at least not until all the fears and broken feelings were fixed and resolved. This was the beginning of another downward spiral, like Alice falling into the rabbit hole toward Wonderland, except that I was falling into *horror-land.*

It felt completely disorienting and bewildering. My wild monkey mind had been triggered again. Time and space was distorted, and all my fears turned into dragons and demons. They were the guardians of my subconscious that I needed in order to subdue and conquer. Like playing Whac-A-Mole, when I thought I had overcome one fear, another one surfaced. When I patched one hole, another part of the emotional pipe leaked. When I put out a fire, another one ran amok. Here I was, keeping the wheel of spiritual undoing running, perhaps till the end of time.

"Will it ever end?" I lamented out loud.

The presence of the beautiful beach houses in Encinitas suddenly became insulting to me. It was driving me to madness, and I had to run before I lost myself. For someone with the ability to exercise self-control, usually I was able to calm down and push all these feelings down.

But that night, I ran.

I ran as fast as my legs could go.

I wanted my lungs to burn out and my arteries to blow up, wishing that I would be able to somehow pass out.

I wanted to forget all my pain.

What was I doing walking around this idyllic neighborhood contemplating my existential crises, anyway?

After all that running, I found an empty bench that was in proximity to the beach. By then, it was pitch-black out, and I immediately felt the comfort of the darkness; the nothingness suited me. I sat there feeling the soothing breeze from the ocean while catching my breath.

And in that brief moment, a spark of insight lit up inside me as I remembered something that I had read in the book *Radical Acceptance* by Tara Brach. She shared that Milarepa had dealt with his inner demons not by running away or fighting them, but by surrendering his head to the demon's mouth. He practiced this complete surrender not out of victimhood but by experiencing the demon directly and wakefully. When he did so, all his demons vanished, and what remained was the brilliant light of pure awareness.

Recalling such a story, I whispered, "Maybe I could be a Milarepa too."

As I stared into the abyss, I decided not to run away from myself anymore. I had finally found the courage to process the angst that was haunting every step of my sauntering. And so, I sat there, closed my eyes, paid attention to my breath, and directed my awareness within. I decided to find out if Milarepa's strategy of putting one's head into the demon's mouth was actually effective.

The journey inward felt like peeling an onion, layer by layer. Onions stink and sting. Likewise, behind each memory was another memory, and behind each buried feeling was another feeling that I never knew was there. Many times, I thought I had gotten over something, only to later realize that I hadn't. I learned the hard way that it was better not to rush the process. The timing of it wasn't even up to me to begin with.

I learned to let the dust settle through meditation classes. I remembered that all I had to do was be a bystander in my own mind. Meditation was like watching a movie in my own head. However, whatever I was experiencing was more than just a visual experience—it was multidimensional and multisensorial. Watching my own mind sent a cascade of emotions churning through my body. There were memories that came in various forms of sound; there was music, words spoken by others, and all the thoughts that I had wrestled with before. Behind those thoughts were hidden fears and desires.

And again, I found myself with a strong desire to run, to do something about these strong feelings, to not just sit there, but to act right away. I felt the need for an outlet, and I wanted to prove to the world how broken everything was.

How could people continue to be in so much denial about things?

How is it possible for people to continue life as business as usual?

My mind was like a train that sped off into an abyss, and I forgot that there was even a bench. I don't know how long I spent ruminating on my inner rage, but it was suddenly interrupted by a flash of awareness, reminding me of my original intention.

Just be here.

Just be here.

Just be here.

Each time my mind returned to the present, I was able to experience the expansion of my awareness encompassing the totality of the environment. The sounds of the ocean came back, the bench that I sitting on felt more tangible, and my breath felt longer and deeper.

There was spaciousness in between my thoughts, and there was a sense that everything was a part of me. It was a glorious experience that I decided to call *loving awareness*, and it had the capacity to love everything and anything around me. It was only a momentary experience, but at least I got a glimpse of what it felt like to be free.

The spaciousness of loving awareness was like a vacuum— soon it was ready to be filled up with more thoughts, more memories, more emotions, and more stories. The ebb and flow between loving awareness and the wild monkey mind was an uncomfortable cosmic dance within my consciousness. Nevertheless, I was at least glad that I no longer misunderstood this orderly chaos of my inner thoughts, and I had slowly begun to befriend the nature of my human mind.

The words of singer-songwriter Trevor Hall, from the song "You Can't Rush Your Healing," started to play itself in my mind. He was singing about the dualistic nature of our human experience, and that momentary confusion was a necessary stepping-stone toward clarity. Healing ourselves is never within our own time, but within divine timing that is beyond human comprehension and control.

As helpless as the healing experience felt, it's actually a preparation from the Universe, which has bigger plans for us. Even in times of darkness, the Universe's love is present. The rest is up to us to open our hearts to see and receive that love and Divine Grace.

I was reminded that our mind looks into the world through the light, whereas our heart looks into the world through the darkness. To heal, I intuitively knew that I had to watch my inner and outer worlds with my heart, where the origins of this loving awareness existed. Next, I had to dive deeper into my own darkness to set the truth of the matter free.

And behind the song, a new layer of memories bubbled up.

I remembered sitting in the bathtub listening to Hall's song years ago. I was experiencing another flare-up of my skin, and I needed a bath full of oats to help me soothe the pain. I didn't know if that remedy actually worked to ease the symptoms, but soaking in a body of water at least helped me loosen the tension I was holding on to.

I never asked to have this pain. Before I had the ability to make conscious decisions in my life, I had already developed this autoimmune skin condition.

Why did this have to happen?

Why me?

Why did this condition not disappear for good when treated with medicine?

Why was I so different from other people?

I remembered sobbing with self-pity, feeling unloved and unwanted, thinking that I was somehow destined to live a cursed life. I didn't understand why there were no solutions or answers when we were living in an era where science and technology were flourishing.

Was I really being punished by God?

And the worst part was that I had to hide my pain, because expressing it to those around me felt wrong. I knew I needed to relinquish it once and for all.

"How did all of this start?" I asked now, exhaling with a sigh that was probably loud enough for any passerby to hear. I only dared allow that to happen because I knew it was already close to midnight, and no one was around.

At this point, only streetlights and the dim crescent moon lit up the bench I was sitting on. In that lonely hour, I continued to seek answers from the inner demon's mouth.

I thought about my parents and how challenging it had been to raise a difficult child like me. Until this point, I had only thought about my condition from my perspective. Now, I felt bad for troubling my parents. I wished that I had been normal, just like any other kid, and maybe they could have had an easier life. As far as I was able to remember, I had special needs, but I had loving parents who were dedicated to meeting them.

Nevertheless, that kind of love was sort of imposed upon me. No one had asked me if I needed special diets, a clean bed every week, or an air-conditioned room in the first place. I never did ask for those special treatments, and some basic needs were also denied.

I wasn't allowed to play or exercise too much because sweating exacerbated my skin inflammation.

I wasn't allowed to sit in the sun, because apparently, sunlight was damaging to my skin.

I wasn't allowed to eat what others were eating because those foods caused harm to me and not them.

Most of this advice was given to me by doctors and adults who thought they knew better. I felt invalidated, as if everyone saw me as a problem to be fixed. As a child, I found that inconvenient and annoying because suddenly it was as if I had a spotlight with a motion detector following my every move. My parents' eyes were on me like a hawk.

Worst of all, for some reason, when I received those special treatments, there were people who were jealous. Their jealousy pushed me away, and I found myself progressively becoming more distant from others. Special treatments felt more like a torture than a luxury. Perhaps if I was given those basic human needs in the first place, then I wouldn't have had these special needs.

What I needed was human connection; and for my creativity and authenticity to be seen, heard, and acknowledged.

What I needed was a safe space where I could throw tantrums, and then learn that emotions didn't need to dictate my every choice.

What I needed was to fall and fail and not be overly protected so that I could have been more resilient in response to life's unavoidable pain.

What I needed was to play with mud, sand, and the grass so my body could have been able to develop some immunity on its own.

Too bad that when I was a child, I didn't have the voice or consciousness to ask for these things. Too bad that my parents were in the dark and didn't really know how to raise a hypersensitive child like me.

But despite all of it, I knew that my parents loved me, and I was grateful that they had done what they could for me. Yet, I felt guilty even *thinking* that they didn't do enough for me. Sometimes being human means that we have to deal with conflicting emotions at the same time.

I wondered what happened to my family before I developed this condition. I remembered that before everything went downhill with my health, I used to live healthily and normally. I was like any other child.

How did all of this change so suddenly?

I noticed that there was a gap in my memory before and after I was diagnosed with the autoimmune skin condition. Something might had happened that my consciousness didn't want to remember. Knowing the body, nothing is really forgotten, only pushed aside temporarily. Just because I wasn't conscious of it didn't mean it wasn't there.

Perhaps there was more than what met my eyes.

CHAPTER THREE

Broken Before Life
Even Started

Feeling stuck in my process, I opened my eyes and looked up to the sky to seek guidance as to what to do next. My eyes caught the constellation Orion easily. The three stars in the middle that formed Orion's belt were easily identifiable. And along the same linear trajectory, if I could have drawn a line with a ruler in the sky, I would have found another star that I held close to my heart—the brightest star in the night sky: Sirius.

The big blue star was my wishing star because of its luminosity and presence in the night sky. Every time I peered at Sirius and made a connection to it, there was a deep sense of familiarity and belonging. I didn't really stop to wonder why that was so. This was another mystery that I hoped would be revealed to me one day. As I gazed toward Sirius, I felt called to bring this process to the Universe for divine guidance.

I had no memory of when or how I first began talking to the Universe or where I picked up this private ritual. No one had taught me, but I intuitively knew how to have these conversations with the Universe, especially when I got stuck.

There was little to no guidance from people around me when it came to answering the existential questions I was so curious about. Or more practically, no one was able to engage in a dialogue with me about questions related to deep suffering in our human experience that I urgently needed answers to. As such, I learned to be my own resource by splitting my consciousness into two, where one represented the parent or the teacher within, and another represented the ignorant and helpless inner child.

This made me feel a little bipolar, because both voices had to come through my same mind. Practicing this private ritual often enough, though, helped me understand that my mind worked like a radio transmitter. Depending on which frequency I tuned in to, I was able to receive different cues. If I stayed in fear-based thinking, I would only be able to receive fear-based solutions. However, if I raised the frequency to see, feel, hear, and experience the world with love, I'd be able to receive insights and creative solutions that were loving and empowering.

I practiced by asking my mind really profound questions and attuning myself to the higher frequencies of love, peace, and harmony. Some of my favorite questions were:

What would love do in this moment?

What is the good here that I'm not seeing right now?

What is the first best step I can take right now to be in love, peace, and harmony?

By personifying my perspective of life from those higher vibrations, I was able to receive wisdom and insight that

I otherwise wasn't able to find from books or people. This was exactly what Albert Einstein had figured out—*we cannot solve a problem with the same mind that created it in the first place.* So the commonsense solution is to solve it with a different mind!

Sometimes the answers didn't come right away, and sometimes they did. The game was how much trust I was able to give the Universe, how much space I was able to create in my mind, and how much love and compassion I was able to give myself in the moment. When I was able to meet these three requirements, inspiring insights and wisdom always landed on my doorstep. This made me believe that we all already have the answers within us, especially when we're able to ask the right questions.

There was also a peculiar way in which the Universe loved to communicate with me. Through meaningful coincidences and the tug and pull of my heart, the Universe pointed me in the right direction. It usually knocked on my heart's door with an invitation, and all that was left was my heart's willingness to say yes.

The decision of my heart was usually spontaneous and immediate. And what came after that was a rumbling urge from my gut. If it was tense, then it was a red light, and I had to be careful. If it was loose and relaxed, then it was a green light, and I could go for it.

During my many sauntering experiences, I had been building sensitivity in order to be conscious of the language of my heart through my body. I had learned to notice subtle changes in my core—whether it was tense or whether it was relaxed.

Sometimes my core stayed silent.

Sometimes an energetic chill spiraled up and down my spine.

39

Sometimes my face flushed with heat.

Sometimes my ears heard ringing sounds at a high vibration, which only I was able to hear.

Sometimes my muscles twitched involuntarily.

Getting to know these different sensations was all about learning how my body was able to respond to subtler stimuli. It sounded animalistic, but when they all came together—along with my neutral and receptive mind—they became the unified voice of my heart. This was exactly like being in an orchestra where all the instruments came together as one to create a harmonic and melodious sound. As for my bodily instrument, these sensations came together in resonance to deliver an inner knowing from my soul.

Always to my delight, when I trusted my heart, the results filled me with wonder. Most of the time, I found myself to be in *kairos*, a Greek word that essentially means "being in the right place at the right time, doing the right thing." My heart became a compass that I learned to fully trust, despite the contradictory and conflicting ideological battles of my rational mind. I found that my logical mind was limited in perception, and the voice of my heart usually cut through dualistic thinking. Eventually, I learned that the existence of synchronicity and meaningful coincidences was a message from the Universe's waking intelligence, which was conscious of the voice of my heart.

As I continued to gaze at Sirius, I felt called upon to reflect on the events that had led up to my birth. Without further ado, I entertained that tug curiously and slid my hand into my pocket to take out my phone, swiped up at the screen to unlock it, and searched for the astrology app that I had downloaded to access my natal birth chart.

This came in handy, because peering into my birth chart felt like looking into the mirror of my consciousness. My study of astrology had revealed many insights about the forces that were at play when I was born. It helped me ask the right questions and led my process of inquiry in the right direction. I was constantly fascinated by how these forces were able to continually impact my development, even after decades of change and growth.

How astrology worked challenged my tiny analytical mind. But, with respect to my cosmic mind, there was an inner knowing, and it made perfect sense.

And as for my gut, it was a green light.

I was born four days after the convergence of the sun, the moon, and the earth on the ecliptic plane. When those luminaries aligned in a straight line, a majestic celestial phenomenon had occurred: a solar eclipse. An influx of energy had been focused and channeled onto planet Earth, like shining light energy through a magnifying glass onto one spot. This was a time of divine intervention, a space of total chaos-in-order and unforeseen circumstances beyond the control of any human efforts.

Many ancient traditions referred to eclipses as ominous phenomena rife with superstitions and bad omens. Ancient myths told that during eclipses, a disruption of human activities through natural disasters happened tragically—bad luck, crises, and other types of misfortune emerged during these times. There were stories told about threshold guardians such as dragons, mystical beasts, demons, and jealous gods of the heavens who were blamed for stealing the sun to usurp its power. Besides that, many had believed that eclipses were harmful to a pregnant woman, and a child born under these stars was cursed—and seen as a symbol of a bad omen. Consequently, people who lived in the past performed many rituals and ceremonies with the intention of chasing away those demonic figures to make offerings to restore their sun, and to provide blessings and protection for a child born under the influence of the eclipse.

How much of these rationales were sensible, though?

When we lack the knowledge to understand such occurrences, it's normal for humans to be afraid. As a result, we have developed defenses that might be exaggerated. Many millennia ago, losing light in the middle of the day was indeed terrifying to human beings, when we didn't have any actual understanding of astronomical phenomena. In ancient cultures, the sun and the moon were worshipped as divine objects of the sky and sacred entities of our world. Something like an eclipse must have been very disorienting. Despite much progress in scientific knowledge of these phenomena, our present-day emotional experiences still get distorted. Moreover, the intensity of disorientation can be heightened.

Why, then, even with an understanding of what is happening, do we get disoriented on such an emotional and primal level?

The ancients knew that the gravity of such a phenomenon was beyond just a physical experience of losing light during the day. Symbolically, eclipses were indeed a time of blindness, of surrendering human intervention to give way to the forces of the Universe. Maybe those myths were created with the goal of restoring the alignment of our human journey with the greater harmony of life through genuine humility. The ancients knew that it was a time of rewriting what was in their original script, and that eclipses were opportunities to renew their souls' contracts with the Universe. In doing so, there was the possibility of transforming the darkness of the eclipse into light. It was to experience the Divine Grace of the Universe in the land of the human realm.

On that subject, it was also said that many great kings and queens of the world were born and died during these eclipse portals, which offered a destined path of great promise for souls to have an all-encompassing influence on the world.

Some succeeded and some failed.

Nevertheless, they were the ones who held an immense presence in the world, leaving crucial and important marks on what was to come next, for better or for worse.

So, am I destined to be a bad omen for the world?

Or am I destined to have great promise and rise up into the world like a king?

I was told that a series of unfortunate events occurred right up until my birth. My mother and I were matched up with an irresponsible obstetrician who prioritized his needs over his patients'. We were scheduled for the delivery according to *his* availability, and my mother was advised to be drugged to speed up the delivery date. I was scheduled for a specific date so that the doctor could go on his holiday and return to deliver me. This was one of the normal things about our overly domesticated modern human culture that ignored the organic process of nature.

Nonetheless, it seemed that the Universe had a different plan for my birth.

Leading up to my birth, my mother had a serious asthma attack, which was of concern to everyone in our family. A pregnant woman with difficulty breathing needed to be hospitalized and carefully monitored. She was close to delivering me, so my family wanted to avoid any mishaps. Taking precautionary measures, she arrived the hospital in the evening and was injected with strong pharmaceutical drugs to relieve her asthmatic condition. That was the beginning of corticosteroid prescriptions for both of us. The drugs did wonders in effectively easing her symptoms; however, this came along with many side effects that weren't explicitly disclosed. Overcome by fear and anxiety, my parents barely had time to make any informed decisions or ask about these side effects. They had absolute trust in the hospital and in the medical authorities, having faith that the best care would be administered.

The protocol was to treat the most urgent problem, and that was inarguable.

So, after the doctors soothed my mother's asthmatic flare-up, she was sent home without any further observation, despite having a delivery date that was imminent. But it didn't take too long for the pharmaceutical drugs to kick in, especially since they had been administered in such high doses. It also didn't take long for me to let my mother know that I wanted to be delivered immediately. The same night, after returning from the hospital for a couple of hours, my mother had to come back to deliver me.

It was already close to midnight when preparations were completed for my delivery. This unforeseen circumstance interfered with the obstetrician's initial plan, however, and he was unavailable to be present for my delivery. My mother and

I were in the hands of the nurses who were working after hours that night. Midway through labor, the pain was too much for my mother to bear and also stay conscious. Memories of what happened that night are faint for her.

Meanwhile, my father, who had never entered a labor room before, popped in and out anxiously to make sure that everything was all right. He was a cautious man, and as a mechanical engineer, he had a sharp mind. He was ready for any possible crises and never hesitated to seek alternative solutions. So, he was on guard, ready to intervene at any time. He was also sure to get ahold of his brother, who was a doctor, in case any professional advice was needed.

It was not a smooth birth at all. The severance from the womb felt invasive to me. I was stuck and hesitant, not sure if I wanted to stay in or come out. In my own way, I protested that it wasn't time yet. I wasn't ready for this world. There was a lot of push and pull. It was unimaginable how far it stretched my mother physically, emotionally, and spiritually to stay awake and help me get out.

Given my stubborn nature, even then, clearly I didn't like to be pressured into or out of a situation. I always wanted things to happen of my own accord, in my own rhythm, and through my own will. However, if I were to choose between an environment of no control versus the invasive world, I would choose the latter. This was because at least being outside the womb, I was able to learn to be in control.

After a couple of hours through the many tides and waves of pushing and pulling, I was out. My first battle as a separate individual was initiated. As I took my first breath with my new functioning lungs, I let out a cry signifying my existence in this world.

I was already disoriented as a result of the invasive nature of my birth, and extenuating circumstances only made it worse, as I was denied that first touch of nurturance and safety from my mother. Instead, I was washed off by the hands of a stranger who was wearing cold and sterile latex gloves and was left alone in some sort of cubicle-like incubator.

As for my mother's situation, the obstetrician finally arrived and was working on her because she was bleeding uncontrollably. He was tempted to take the easy way out by cutting the womb off along with her future womanhood and sealing the wound. She was put into a life-and-death situation. After she delivered me, she recalled that she was close to passing out, with the white light welcoming her consciousness.

As for my father, he remembers being agitated and concerned. He immediately contacted his brother and made sure that he intervened by connecting him to the obstetrician working on my mother. The obstetrician was at least open to listening to another opinion, and went along with the task of massaging my mother's womb until she naturally stopped bleeding. After all that arduous effort, she was cleaned up, and her condition stabilized.

It wasn't until a couple of days later that we reunited as mother and son. Of course, I have no recollection of what happened during that time, but I have no doubt that this experience left a mark on me of abandonment, insecurity, and pain that metastasized into my subconscious.

After all, the body always keeps score.

Over the years, my parents and I tended to regard this event as a normal birth. It wasn't until the present that I began to reconcile this painful memory with my current life. Hearing the ocean crashing into the shore at a distance, there was a resounding call for me to heal my inner brokenness. But I intuitively knew that the severity of my birth trauma was beyond my capacity to heal, and the timing of this healing wouldn't be up to me.

Recalling my birth story, I recognized that I harbored deep-rooted anger that had become a raging river that I didn't know how to navigate. It was irrational, and there was no one to point my finger at. Growing up, I had been mostly angry at nothing, and until now, I never understood why I felt the way I did.

I was just angry!

I felt rejected and unworthy to be alive. This world that I incarnated into didn't feel safe for me. Irrationally, maybe this was why I found people around me and life in general to be untrustworthy and unreliable. All I had was myself, and I intended to keep it that way. I saw how it made perfect sense that I turned into someone who needed to take control of every aspect of my life. I armored myself like an armadillo, trying to avoid any instances of vulnerability or loss of control.

With such extreme coping, I felt victimized and vengeful, because I didn't choose to be this way. Hence, true love was something I wasn't able to truly and fully believe in.

Yes, I had been broken before life even started for me. It was a brokenness that had never been able to be fixed up until now—a broken glass that could never become unshattered.

And I couldn't help but wonder: *Did other people feel as broken as I was, coming into this world?*

CHAPTER FOUR

The Divine Grace
of the Universe

I t was time to consult the Universe. "Why was I born in such a dramatic fashion?"

"Everything that is done unto you or done unto this world, is done out of love and compassion," whispered the Universe into my mind after a long pause.

"Wait, what?" I protested in disbelief. I was unable to accept that deep pain and suffering was the way of the world.

Is the Universe trying to say that behind these experiences lie love and compassion?

I refused to see life in such a way, but at least I was open enough to contemplate the subject. From within, I was burning with the absolute conviction to get to the bottom of what the Universe had said, no matter how uncomfortable and inconvenient it was. I just wanted to discover the truth.

Being clear with my intention, I began my inquiry process:

What is the good here that I'm not seeing?
What is the good here that I'm not seeing?
What is the good here that I'm not seeing?

I repeated the question again and again, and I was committed to sitting on that bench until I found my answers. Slowly the background of my environment began to fade, and I started to dive deep into my consciousness, getting lost in profound thoughts.

The first question that popped into my mind was: *Is there such a thing as true love and compassion?*

During my life, up until this time, I had experienced expressions of love and compassion that felt more like mere lip service that people spouted every now and then. People's interactions and exchanges—be they acts of service, words of affirmation, giving and receiving gifts, physical contact, or spending quality time with others—all seemed empty and hollow to me. They felt more like they were coated with hidden agendas that were birthed out of unfulfilled emotional needs and insecurity. I felt that people were behaving in this way because deep down, we all felt inherently unworthy and undeserving. Love felt as if we were latching on to each other through mutual parasitism, holding each other down just to uphold our own neuroses.

I hypothesized that the reason behind it all was that we were all collectively having unnatural birth experiences that had been deemed normal in modern society. Epidurals, C-sections, labor inductions, sanitized environments in birth rooms, incubators, and many innovative interventions geared to support the labor process were all well and good, but had anyone thought to consider how these interventions were impacting the human soul? Birth was definitely not just about getting the baby's body out of the mother. It was also a sacred ceremony initiating a human soul to enter the physical world.

I believed that all souls incarnating into this world expected to be treated with genuine love, respect, and safety. Yet, it felt like I had entered a world that was filled with ignorance, aggression, and aversion, where most of us were caught up in a delusional fantasy of superficial love that was empty and hollow. It seemed like the ugliness of human negativity was a disclaimer in fine print that I didn't see when I agreed to incarnate on Earth.

In this delusional world, I discovered two types of people: the realists and the idealists.

Realists were the types of people who were in denial about the existence of true love. They pushed it away and numbed their lives with addictive and intoxicating stimulants and activities.

Some had the impression that they were larger than life.

Some were busy keeping up with the status quo.

And some decided to build empires.

Underneath all those grandiosities was a hurt that they were so afraid to recognize and feel. Overcommitting, overtraining, and overworking became acceptable social norms for them, and these habits were further perverted into celebrated qualities. These behaviors manifested as addictions of the mind and intoxications of the soul, which eventually led to the breaking down of the body.

Right, that was me.

As for the idealists, they were making castles in the sky about how love was all about sweet and fluffy experiences, expecting their problems to simply vanish on their own. Many were not willing to plough the murky mud of their psyches;

they expected to automatically taste the fruits of spiritual freedom and creative growth. But if they had been able to put an end to pain, fear, and stress altogether, they would have done so already.

The ones saving others and the ones waiting to be saved were both at the ends of the same idealist spectrum. The ones constantly saving others saw the world as broken, focusing on the suffering of others because deep down they were afraid to face their own personal wounds.

Wait a moment—that was me too!

Then, there were those who were constantly waiting to be saved, living in denial, and expecting some divine power greater than they were to take their suffering away.

Just like me!

The saviors and the victims made great pairs, and together, they danced in a toxic relationship of emotional and spiritual abuse. Seeing the world in such consciousness, love and compassion became an incomplete philosophy to escape from the intensity of their very own suffering. Those who treaded such paths were like flies who were drawn to the light, only ending up being electrocuted.

These perspectives were conditioned deep within me. The realist was that part of me who wanted to fight, who wanted to prove, and who wanted to be righteous about what I thought was best in order to live a worthwhile life. And the idealist was that part of me who was in a state of flight and freeze. I wanted to run away and to numb out. I was constantly feeding myself with lies that were too convenient to be the truth so that the suffering of life was bearable.

Ultimately, these worldviews were an attempt to love truthfully, but they barely described the truth of the matter.

They were nothing but a subjective reflection of the reptilian and primal parts of my autonomic nervous system that was programmed, designed, and made for survival. Of course, fear had to come first. We were all loving out of fear.

Ah, me too!

Fearful and unconscious behavior in the name of love perpetuated more separation than connection. When I offered love accompanied by fear, I became controlling and domineering, always expecting someone else to reciprocate that love. When I received love with fear, I became shameful and unworthy, always assuming that the other person was giving me transactional love out of ulterior motives. Neither path had ever created harmony within me or in my relationships. And most damaging of all, I wasn't able to be aware of that sort of behavior, or if did, I didn't know why I had even allowed those behaviors to occur in the first place.

However, when I gave myself the chance to experience this situation from the perspective of my body, it made complete sense. Protection and safety had to come first for the primal nervous system, even if they weren't the most skillful or ideal solutions. I simply maladapted from this misperception, and it wasn't a choice. What wasn't a choice, then, wasn't an action, but a reaction of the subconscious mind.

Great intention, silly execution.

Nevertheless, that wasn't where I was supposed to stop. Learning from biology, humans are not made simply to survive, but to thrive. I just needed to know how my biology was able to serve me rather than going against me all the time.

Otherwise, what was the point of such a powerful and evolved prefrontal cortex?

There existed another pathway in the nervous system that

was able to reteach our fearful and unconscious behaviors, and that involved the use of our prefrontal cortex of our mammalian brain. I'd always regarded the prefrontal cortex as the programmer of our human system. And as the programmer of that system, it was not only able to rationalize our fears, but also to ultimately choose love and compassion in the face of fear to become the best version of who we are.

This was why I believed what writer and teacher Stephen Jenkinson once said: "Human beings are not born. Human beings are made." It wasn't my fear that defined me, but what I chose in the face of fear. Fear had given me an awareness of what wasn't working well, and with that awareness, I had the chance to go beyond my limitations.

Fundamentally, I was truly seeking the path of love.

Birth is the beginning of the path of love, and it's never without the presence of fear.

The truth was that in order to walk the path of love, I had to walk toward and through the experiences of fear. *I had to understand that everything done unto us and unto the world is done out of love and compassion.* Just like what the Universe had shared with me.

These worldviews of the realist and the idealist were just temporary training wheels in coping with the complexity of the world and the dynamic reality of this Universe. They were only two pieces of the puzzle of how I was able to experience life. Without one or the other, I would have struggled to make sense of our human experience. At the same time, if I had never taken those training wheels off, I would have never removed myself from the pain and suffering of duality. Life was never an "either-or" situation, but rather, a "both-and-beyond" situation.

And to take those training wheels off, I had to saunter into the unknown, risking every comfort that I had built up over the years of my life, and confront fear to get to the truth of the matter. For this, I was grateful for my truth-seeking spirit and the wildness of my humanity that had dared me to go beyond the confines of such a duality to find my peace within the unknown.

If only I had known about this earlier!

This was why birth or simply existing was an overwhelming experience. Life didn't come with a set of manuals from the Universe. Up to this time in history, humanity has only attempted to write manuals on how we *understand* life. Bibles, scriptures, and sacred texts are the human interpretations of the divine. It was bewildering before we had these stories that informed our world. Yet, in the attempt to create these concepts of our existence, we lost touch with the true essence of the world.

Like most of us, I experienced a form of amnesia. My individual consciousness was separated from the unity consciousness when I was born. And the journey of life was such that I came in with love and compassion—only to forget about those qualities through fearful life experiences of pain and suffering—and then making a full circle by remembering once more the true essence of love in the presence of pain and suffering.

Love was incomplete if I wasn't able to embrace fear.

I used to think that I was broken because of such a separation, but this was a complete misperception. There was no denying the pain of my past experiences, but just because I was in pain, completely confused and bewildered, it didn't mean that I was broken.

There are two types of pain: the unavoidable pain of the human experience that comes through the phenomena of birth, death, sickness, loss, and old age; and the avoidable pain of getting in the way of myself by creating false meaning out of the initial pain.

The irony is that the avoidable pain is caused by my hard-wired denial of the initial pain!

As an infantile human, I had spent most of my suffering dealing with the latter type of pain. Unbeknownst to me, my humanity was all designed for the initial type of pain. There existed a form of resilience within me to turn any adversities into my greatest growth. That resilience was an intelligence of nature that, in the face of pressure, was activated by dormant creative potential. This is exactly how caterpillars turn into butterflies, and seeds turn into beautiful flowers. And in the very same way, this was how my first pain was transmuted into a greater purpose by the Divine Grace of the Universe.

I was far more powerful than I thought, and my entire life up until this point, I had sold myself short.

I saw that the inconvenient truth of birth is the first pain that is part of the journey of any human experience. I had been nothing but a cell in this entire organism that was the cosmos. Birth had been a terrifying process, but it had not been there to victimize me. The world around me had never been broken. Instead, it was my own interpretation of my human experience and the world that was broken.

That was how I got stuck!

I didn't experience life as it was, but as I made it up to be.

My source of pain and suffering was never out there—it was within me all along!

The true spiritual journey, then, was not about transcending anywhere, but about befriending the full spectrum of my human experience within the initial pain, starting with those experiences I had denied, judged, avoided, and repressed. To be reconnected to my true essence, I had to learn to radically accept all aspects of my life.

Moreover, there was no way for me to quantify the odds of my existence. I once read that the probability of incarnation and existing was like finding a needle in the Sahara Desert. There were way too many forces in the Universe that needed to come together at the right time, at the right place, and with the right people, to create just the right moment for me to exist. And I was only one of us, out of more than seven billion humans on Earth.

Never in history have there been so many humans.

Never in history has there been so much potential about to unleash itself on this planet.

Wow! My birth was actually a miracle, and I had forgotten the sacredness of my existence.

My birth was definitely not a mistake. It was what it was and what it had to be.

Leaning closer to the truth of the matter, I felt warmth from the core of my belly starting to radiate throughout my body. I felt a sense of renewal, of hope and inspiration, and this was probably what courage meant viscerally.

Courage is not the absence of fear, but the choices I make in the presence of fear.

Courage is not unequivocal strength, but the willingness to show up in times of weakness.

Courage is fierce love and compassion in action, which is all about witnessing the living experience as it is and taking full responsibility for all that is present.

I knew this deep in my bones—this was the courage that was going to get me through this journey of radically accepting the fundamental pain and suffering of a human incarnation.

Courage is the simple act of witnessing our human experience, similar to how Milarepa put his head into the demon's mouth. Fixated judgments had only bred cycles of ignorance and separation, consequently taking me away from my sacred connection to love and healing.

The greatest gift I was able to give myself and the world was the courage to love myself and to be ordinarily *me* in the presence of others, completely naked and raw. It meant I had to be here on planet Earth and accept the full spectrum of my human experiences, fully and totally. Perhaps this was the starting point of how I was able to begin my healing journey.

As insights continued to stream into my consciousness, I found deeper clarity about my existential angst. Inner peace began to emerge, and both my body and soul progressively felt reenergized and renewed.

I assumed that I was in some kind of non-ordinary state of consciousness where I was able to contemplate difficult circumstances and find higher meaning out of my pain. It felt like there was a floodgate of information entering my mind, as if there was a Wi-Fi network of the Universe that I was able to tune in to. And this network contained all the knowledge of the Universe, which helped me access wisdom and perspectives that I was never able to figure out on my own. All the books, articles, lectures, podcasts, and YouTube videos that I had ever read, watched, or listened to bombarded my mind all at once. And for a brief moment, I experienced a dose of enlightenment and a moment of what it felt like to be *Homo luminous*.

When the emotional turmoil completely shifted and dissipated, I realized that I was gifted with the Divine Grace of the Universe. I was grateful to know that I was being watched over by a higher presence. When I called out for guidance, I received the answers I needed.

Not knowing how much time had passed, I got up from the bench and decided to make my way home. By then, only the night insects' orchestra echoed through the streets, and the calmness of the night soothed my soul.

PART TWO

Conditioning:
The Courage to Remember

*"People say that what we're all seeking is a meaning for life.
I don't think that's what we're really seeking. I think that
what we're seeking is an experience of being alive, so that
our life experiences on the purely physical plane will have
resonances within our own innermost being and reality, so
that we actually feel the rapture of being alive."*

—Joseph Campbell, *The Power of Myth*

CHAPTER FIVE

A Journey of Remembrance

I was in the middle of nowhere.

I had nowhere to run.

Nowhere to escape.

Nowhere to hide.

Nowhere was now, here.

There was no way to escape from myself. It was too late.

The moment I signed up to be off the grid and step into the middle of the jungle, I knew that there was no distraction left to avoid facing my inner demons. I was on Mount Larapata Hatunpata, a pristine and ancient mountain that had been a cradle of Incan and pre-Incan civilizations for thousands of years.

On one side stood the magnificent Andean ranges of mountain, and on the other side was the mysterious emerald-green Amazonian rainforest. I was told that it was an ancient Incan trail (Capagñan) into Paititi (the enlightened realm), which conquistadors had failed to discover. Many had attempted and gotten lost in the maze of nature. Without a guide, there was only a one-way entry. As for the indigenous people of the land, it was a place where they sought refuge and protection, as well as one where they could revere the Great Spirit.

In the middle of the plant-medicine ayahuasca ceremony, I asked myself: *What the hell am I doing here?*

Maybe I had caught the wave of Western New Age spirituality. After spending three years in Boulder, Colorado, I was completely *hippie-fied*. Originally a city boy, I became a lover of nature. I once wore suits and ties to my classes in London. However, after moving to Boulder, I started wearing athleisure clothing for my comfort. Ecstatic dancing, sipping medicinal cacao in ceremonial circles, tarot, crystals, Reiki, astrology, yoga, and meditation had all became normal for me.

Within the New Age community, I had overheard many conversations about chronically dissatisfied people who felt completely disillusioned by the state of the world. And for some reason, the topic of psychedelics and plant-medicine ceremonies was constantly mentioned. Many people claimed that psychedelics and plant medicine were able to help them get closer to their true selves, but I saw how incoherent that claim was. There wasn't actually as much change in their behavior as they claimed. Those who spoke the loudest usually only reflected how distant they were from their true selves.

I became very curious about why that was so. I had found in recent years that research on the hallucinogenic drug DMT (dimethyltryptamine) had taken the main stage in the news. The research on non-ordinary states of consciousness had put psychedelics in the forefront, and there were documentaries out there discussing psychedelics and plant medicine. Applications of psychedelics to treat cases such as PTSD, severe anxiety and depression, and even the optimization of human performance, were discovered. With the backing of science, there was more justification to engage in this form of personal growth and healing. Such psychedelic practices had been used since the ancient days by indigenous people, but it was only in recent times that modern science had caught up.

It was just like with yoga—in that it wasn't until modern science proved its validity that it finally gained acceptance from the public. Naturally, some criticized modern society's hypocrisy in taking credit for, and profiting from, the wisdom of ancient traditions that had been practiced for thousands of years.

Why were indigenous and ancient wisdom practices condemned as barbaric, nonsensical, primitive, or superstitious, only to be found to be enlightening after being certified or proven by modern, Western scientific entities?

While people were busy debating whether there was injustice involved, beyond the righteousness of human morality, the Universe had bigger plans for us. It was thanks to the exposure provided by modern science that people like me had the opportunity to participate in a plant-medicine ceremony.

Deep down, I knew why I was here.

I was searching for medicine for my soul, a place that I was able to call home, and a remedy for the persistent autoimmune skin condition that continued to plague my life despite having tried many holistic-healing interventions. At this point, I figured that my disease was more than what met the naked eye, and that my soul was in distress.

I wanted something comprehensive, pure, and straightforward. I needed a diamond cutter that was able to cut through all the falsehoods and pretentious temptations in an unforgiving yet compassionate way. After window-shopping for various forms of spirituality, I realized that what was being sold often seemed profound and beautifully perfect, but rarely turned out to be what it appeared.

At this point in my spiritual growth, my body had developed a sniper's accuracy and precision with respect to intuition. It always knew what was too good to be true, but my mind had trouble catching up with that intuition. Each time I approached new spiritual modalities, my body responded by being sick to the core, as if sounding an alarm that all that glitters was not gold. Despite that, I caved in to the attraction and gave my energy away repeatedly, bringing myself closer to greater disillusionment.

In my search for a remedy, I used myself as a lab rat to experiment with different spiritual and healing modalities. Most of the time, I was curious, but deep down, I knew that I was desperate. Consequently, I ended up getting hurt. I became a consumer of spirituality and, as a result, I became a target for energetic predators. Even though I knew that what these ill-intended perpetrators did was wrong, I never did protect myself or confront them. I felt that it was inconvenient to burst the bubble. I was afraid to create conflict and feared being ostracized or cursed with "black magic" if I spoke out.

So I turned a blind eye.

New Age spirituality offered ways to hack through our lives so that spiritual gold was seemingly able to be attained quickly. Instead of digging deep into cultivating proper values and working on foundational steps to reform one's lifestyle and habits, many thought they could gain immediate gratification by being "spiritual."

Many of us had built ivory towers and castles in the sky. And when the darkness of Earth's reality confronted us, our murky dark sides showed up and engulfed us. Not only did we hurt ourselves, but with our greater power, we inflicted greater damage on those around us.

Spirituality became a dogma that informed our narrow worldview and justified our sense of righteousness. It became the next object for human exploitation. Chögyam Trungpa, a Tibetan Buddhist teacher, cleverly summarized this phenomenon as "spiritual materialism."

Instead of mindlessly accumulating material wealth, people turned to a quest for spiritual power. Greed and exploitation were still involved. The form of our pursuit might have changed, but in the end, by playing this game, we were all still trapped within our own ignorance and misperception.

We might have gained insights about what freedom and happiness felt like, but until we dug into the trenches of our unproductive habits, true liberation wouldn't be possible. The real work—reforming the core limiting beliefs that carved deep into our stubborn subconscious programming, having difficult conversations in triggering relationships, and befriending the darkest parts of our human experiences—needed to be done. The integration and embodiment of our spiritual ideas had to be followed through in our everyday behaviors and be reflected in our choices.

Without such a process, spirituality looked like fancy wings that weren't able to take flight. As such, the wear and tear between spirit and body deepened. True spirituality had always been about uniting spirit and matter, which meant experiencing the full spectrum of human experience and acting from unconditional love despite the presence of pain, fear, and stress in our bodies and in our lives.

I knew about the dangers of setting forth into an unknown land, being in the middle of nowhere. I also knew about the risks of putting myself in a space where my consciousness would be left unguarded.

Despite all that, I made a commitment to surrender completely to the elements of nature that were as foreign to me as the strangers sitting next to me in this ceremony. There was no promise that this adventure would be able to cure my disease.

Yet I was drawn to it.

Even with its uncertain outcome, I was called upon to step into this adventure. The unforeseen future was captivating and alluring. The chance to potentially discover something new was exciting. What nailed my decision was the ineffable knowing that I was being guided and taken care of.

There was that green light again, both from the heart and the gut.

Leading up to the plant-medicine ceremony, I made sure that I consulted with, and confided in, trustworthy friends and mentors who knew the language of the heart, as well as those who had participated in psychedelic journeys. I needed extra confirmation and support to make an informed decision, just to be safe.

It all began when I accidentally eavesdropped on a conversation about plant medicine. That initiated a desire and curiosity within me, which led me to a connection with a friend from university. She prepared me by showing me a documentary, and was generous in sharing her personal experiences with plant medicine. Through our conversations, new ideas blossomed, which led me to walk the path less traveled.

Such inspiration then led me to moments of synchronistic decisions. This is how, in a flicker of a moment, I found myself at the Paititi Institute in the middle of the Peruvian jungle. I was a six-hour drive away from the nearest city of Pisac, and then had to take a four-hour hike into the depths of the mountains from the nearest village.

Again, I found myself having an intimate conversation with the Universe.

It had been about two years since our last self-illuminating conversation, which I had told no one about. Only this time, I wasn't the only one. Right in front of me was a group of souls who had come together through a fateful encounter to explore the depths of our being. Because of that, the difficulty level of this challenge had increased twofold.

I didn't just have to open up to the Universe, but also to strangers I didn't know anything about as well. After all, being vulnerable enough to open up to others had never been my forte.

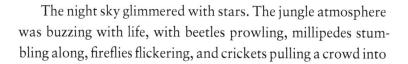

The night sky glimmered with stars. The jungle atmosphere was buzzing with life, with beetles prowling, millipedes stumbling along, fireflies flickering, and crickets pulling a crowd into their nightly practice. In the ceremonial tent, we were all in the middle of the process of meeting "Grandmother Ayahuasca," and were being initiated into a journey of remembrance.

My senses were heightened, and my consciousness expanded in ways that I had never experienced before. With the faculty of sight taken away by the darkness, my other senses were awakened. My senses were heightened so much, in fact, that I felt my blood flowing through my veins and arteries. As I inhaled, I felt spaces in my body that I never knew existed. As I exhaled, I felt electricity flowing and vibrating through the base of my spine to my brain, forming a circular circuit with particles accelerating and ready to collide to form a massive explosion. My auditory attunement to sound amplified to the point that it became too painful to be listening to both the shaman's medicinal music and the insects' accompaniment in the background.

I learned that the shaman's singing in the middle of the ceremony brought medicine to the soul. Depending on what the soul was confronting in the ceremony, the music was able to create a unique experience for each participant.

I discovered that our experience of reality is different from person to person, depending on our perception. We perceive what we believe rather than the actual truth of the matter. Some people thought the music was enjoyable, but I experienced it as disharmonious and disastrous, which left me in distress and pain.

Luckily, it didn't stay that way the whole night. There were also moments when I enjoyed the disharmony. There were the rising and falling waves of both delight and distress throughout the evening, and the only way I could ease my experience was to be in a place of neutrality and equanimity.

I learned very quickly not to indulge in the pleasure and not to resist the pain. I was forced to learn acceptance regardless of what experiences came through. Sitting upright and going back to my breath with intention helped, just like in my meditation practices.

In the midst of deep breathing at one point, I was brought into deeper layers of consciousness. No longer ruminating about existential and philosophical struggles of life, I was brought home to who I was before I was conditioned by the circumstances of this world. It was who I used to be before I became who I thought I had to be through the eyes of others. The image of myself as an infant popped right up into my consciousness. It's an image that I've kept with me in my diary wherever I've gone in my travels. No matter how many times I lost this item, it always uncannily found its way back to me. Amid moments of forgetfulness, this picture showed itself to me, and reminded me to remember who I was.

Deep into my psychedelic experience, I went into a time machine of sorts, where I explored my childlike nature. I never forgot the way my eyes looked as an infant. They were glistening, clear, and shining brightly—reflecting the outer, mysterious world. They were deep and alive, seeming to convey that there was another, alternate reality on the other side. To possess something that was able to remind me of the glow I used to express, when I was just simply being me, was priceless.

But where had all this brilliance gone?

Had I completely lost it?

Or had it just been swept under the rug because of all the painful circumstances that I had to bear witness to, endure, and overcome?

Before I knew it, I became too old and mature for my own age. The innocent eyes that were filled with life and light were taken over by cynical and dubious thoughts of the world. I had completely lost it.

As I traveled forward, I was also moving backward. The journey forward was a process of peeling the layers of protective lies that I had internalized over many years to recover the truth and innocence of the wild child—the wild child who knew what *wonder and ordinary magic* were all about.

Underneath the night of glimmering stars, I remembered the look in my own eyes as an infant.

I remembered what I used to create out of my imagination.

I remembered the burst of creative energy that knew no limits.

I remembered the many memories of waking up each day and looking forward to the exciting adventures of life.

I was an adventurer and an avid explorer of the undiscovered. And my journey forward was about recovering those aspects of myself—a path of remembering my true nature.

CHAPTER SIX

Amid Wonder and
Ordinary Magic

The spirit of the plant medicine whispered to me:
"Play. That is the epitome of your purpose.
"Move. That is the vehicle of your purpose.
"Imagine. That is the exploration of your purpose.
"Curiosity. That is the drive of your purpose.
"Creation. That is the outcome of your purpose.
"Purpose cannot be found, but can be revealed as you live your life fully."

I remembered the mornings in Kuala Lumpur when I was a child. As soon as the velvety-black sky would turn into a beautiful azure hue, my body simply knew that it was time to wake up. Misty clouds usually lingered in the neighborhood overnight, but the moment that birds started to sing, it was time for the clouds to disappear.

Then, from a distance, clapping sounds would emerge and

start to echo across the neighborhood—older people were doing their morning exercises. Every morning, they routinely walked while clapping their hands in the natural rhythm of each arm swing back and forth. I heard that it was an effective way to wake up the bodily system and circulate energy. For me, it was a substitute for the rooster's cock-a-doodle-doo. I didn't care why the adults did what they did—I just thought it was fascinating and rather amusing at the same time.

Waking up in the morning was easy, and I looked forward to it. It was inspiring to see how life began to kick-start, and I wanted to be a part of it. I enjoyed greeting the morning with over-the-top enthusiasm, and I was always open to experiencing life in new ways.

A new day meant a new opportunity to play, to discover, to learn. Whether it was with books or old toys, being in the kitchen, or going outdoors, I had an enormous appetite to participate. I hoped that the adults around me would show me their lives and allow me to join their world. Perhaps today was the day they would consider me old enough to be part of their lives.

My senses were alive, open, clear, and acute. I absorbed everything, I learned quickly, and I could pick up on and express the subtlest details. I was a sensitive, intuitive kid who had a keen taste for food and always looked forward to eating. I constantly sought out contact and touch because it felt essential to me. I spent many hours a day listening to the melodic music of the world with the utmost delight. And building upon that, I quickly learned how to play music via cassette tapes. I was sensitive to blends of color, and I clung to any natural scents because they lightened my spirit. Anything that came from nature made me felt at home in my body. All of these experiences represented the wonder and ordinary magic of my world.

Beyond that, I had an imagination bursting with boundless possibility. I animated the soft toys around me and imbued them with animal spirits, which gave them life that imitated their nature. In return, they offered me companionship and safety. These relationships were important to me, and I took them as seriously as the bonds I had with the people around me. Their companionship was irreplaceable, and they were my friends.

These beings were mostly animals that I felt affection for, seen in the many cartoon characters from TV and in the piles of encyclopedias my father brought home for the family. To connect with my companions, I spent hours and hours looking at the pictures in those books, and along with that was an opportunity to learn their correct names.

Nothing beats being around nature, though. Animated objects were fun and great, but they never could match up to the real deal of having living beings right in front of me. Visiting zoos, bird sanctuaries, and butterfly parks for the first time was delightful. Upon repeated visits, though, I found that the animals in the cages saddened me, whereas those who had space to roam free made me happy. There were many times when I wished for that type of freedom.

Most of the animals I visited minded their own business, but just like I did with the animals in the picture books, I tried to communicate with them. Hence, when any of them decided to pay attention to me or make any attempt to communicate with me, that would make my day. This made me wonder if these parks were made for humans or for animals.

Did the animals amuse me, or was I the one amusing them?

Another fond experience I had while being in nature was looking for fighting spiders in the nearby rubber estate. My father would take my siblings and me to the estate and teach us how to look for these magical beings. After finding them, my father paired them up, and we watched them duel. He also showed us the grasshoppers in the area and taught us which dangers to watch out for. For us city kids, this was about as close to nature as we got.

You see, given the ongoing massive urban development in the area, there simply wasn't much nature left. In fact, it didn't take long for the rubber-tree estate to be taken down and be replaced with a new housing development. Nonetheless, it was enough for me to find wonder and ordinary magic for a brief period of time, even if I just got a glimpse of it.

I was a wild child who wasn't able to sit still. I enjoyed jumping from cushions to cushions, I made pillow fortresses to pounce on, and I watched them fall apart. I spent time running up and down the stairs of our double-story terraced house just to see how fast I could run. In the playground, I climbed on large structures so I could be at a vantage point to overlook the vastness of my small world. I was a daredevil who fearlessly ventured into areas where I wasn't supposed to go. I enjoyed the exhilarating experience of exploring in order to satisfy my vast curiosity.

I also pretended that I knew martial arts and amateurly practiced swinging my limbs and throwing punches around empty spaces. I often imagined myself fighting off opponents who existed in a realm that only I was able to see. This led me to tumble on the floor and try acrobatic stunts clumsily. I was dramatic, and took on everything obsessively by investing all the energy I had.

By the end of the day, I would inevitably fall off my feet and to the ground because I was so tired. I would go to bed filled with satisfaction, looking forward to whatever adventure was going to unfold next.

These were my days of childlike rapture, as I was immersed in my own wonder and ordinary magic.

⸭

My connection to this wonder and ordinary magic was hugely disrupted when rashes that came out of nowhere took over my body, resulting in frequent visits to the doctor. I was diagnosed with chronic atopic dermatitis when I was eight years old, and I was told that I would have to be medicated my entire life because there was no cure for this condition. Consequently, I was given heavy doses of immunosuppressants and antihistamines.

Those drugs were a miracle for me. In the span of less than a week, my symptoms disappeared. However, when I stopped using the medications, my skin symptoms came back in a more aggressive way. My skin's terrible inflammation invaded my body, and taking immunosuppressants was the only solution to put the fire out.

Progressively, it became a vicious and an endless cycle that I had no control over. The fire was never put out; instead, it only grew. I became more dependent on the drugs, and I was close to being a legally and socially approved drug addict. With each visit to the doctor, I was given a heavier dose. Sometimes they would give me something different with a different name, but the purpose was always the same—to suppress the immune system from "overreacting." Hearing explanations from the adults around me always made me feel like I was "too much" and had to be suppressed.

As a growing child, I was hyperactive and constantly bored. I had cravings that drew me to eat foods with lots of carbohydrates, such as wheat, cornflakes, and sweets. I also developed an eating disorder that no one talked about. I was able to eat large amounts of noodles and dumplings, and everybody thought that was normal for a prepubescent kid. This changed for me when doctors ordered a myriad of food-allergy tests that showed I was severely allergic to gluten, seafood, dairy, eggs, and even dust mites.

As a result of these tests, every aspect of my life was controlled and micromanaged by my parents. I was taught that every choice I made affected my health. Everything I did had to be proper: the way I ate, the way I played, the way I behaved, the way I kept my room clean, the way I presented myself, and even the way I groomed myself.

Not long after these new changes in my lifestyle were implemented, I developed another kind of eating disorder where I feared that anything I did or ate was going to attack my skin. I was terribly afraid that I would itch so much that it would lead to wounding myself with scratching. I became overly self-conscious and vigilant about every choice I made in my life. The severity of this was noticeable when I felt that everyone and everything around me was a threat.

Before the diagnosis, I didn't care what the world thought about me; afterward, I started to be afraid to express myself. There was a sense of wrongness in the air. I thought I had to dumb down my authentic expressions of wonder and ordinary magic because apparently they were too loud, too big, and too messy.

When I was having an emotional outburst, instead of being given a safe space to experience my feelings, I was denied this. As a result of that neglect, I learned to swallow experiences of anger and frustration back down in my body, as it was impolite, uncivilized, and unruly to be expressing such volatile emotions. I practiced the art of self-control, and holding myself back became one of those many things I learned to be adept at.

At some point, the bubble of emotions continued to accumulate, and they spoke louder than words through my passive-aggressive body language and mannerisms. Family and friends cheered me on through humor and sarcasm, which further dissociated me from my anger. Sometimes I was greeted with rewards in order to be less emotional, and sometimes I was punished for it. I was also given a lot of lip service to soothe my emotions.

But I didn't feel soothed at all—false positivity was in the air, and I was left with a dark goo of uneasiness within my being. I constantly felt misunderstood and unrecognized if I expressed the truth of my emotions. I felt unseen during my total experience as a human being. The feeling of alienation and being invisible gradually weighed down upon me. I became more perplexed about who I was and more skeptical about the world I was living in. The psychological distress incrementally protruded into my physicality, and I became conspicuously uncomfortable in my own skin.

Unbeknownst to my family and me, such a manifestation was reflecting a diseased and apathetic society that had forgotten what wonder and ordinary magic were. Consequently,

I was constantly seen as an object to be fixed and controlled. Worst of all, I had no idea that all of this was happening in the backdrop of my subconscious, which shaped my identity and personality in the world. I was only an innocent kid.

My skin condition continued to spiral out of control as I grew from a young child into an early adolescent. Along with that, there was something within my consciousness that was expressing the discontent and outrage of my place in the world. It was taking a stand, showing what was dysfunctional not just within me but also around me. It protested:

I want to be seen and accepted for my unique experiences of being human.

I want my sensitivity and empathy to be recognized, soothed, and shown so that these traits are regarded as strengths.

I want to know that my anger is not a threat, but is to be respected as a message that injustice has happened.

I want people to realize that I am made to dance and move, rather than sit obediently in a corner.

I want to be given an opportunity to explore my natural creativity, which is waiting to be discovered and expressed.

I want to stop feeling like I need to be fixed for my brokenness and woundedness.

I want to stop being judged as being childish, imprudent, and immature for having dreams and aspirations.

I want to be free from expectations of perfection and invincibility.

I am not God, and we are not God, so why are we acting like we're supposed to be invincible?

I want to be heard and seen as an ordinary human being.

I need to know if I'm worthy of unconditional love, even if I'm not perfect.

These protests and yearnings went on for years. At first, they were loud and clear. However, as a child, I wasn't able to express them, and no one would have listened even if I had tried. The protestations of a child were always viewed as excuses. Eventually, these voices went quiet and disappeared into my subconscious, as I was heavily medicated with immunosuppressants. The symptoms of my body that were meant to be sacred messengers of my subconscious were silenced. My connection to wonder and ordinary magic started to disappear, and I thought it was normal because I was growing up.

My body and psyche became more robotic, and I became numb to the world. I was cold, disheartened, and disconnected as I battled two demands: one from the voices of the world of what was expected of me, and another from the truthful voice that resided deep within my heart.

Before I knew what was going on, my life got too serious, too quickly. Creative, spontaneous play progressively disappeared from my life, as my responsibilities increased. I was constantly nagged by my parents' stern and anxious overwatch. Play was also interrupted by the solemn routine of academic learning, which became a tedious chore to keep up with. On top of the rules imposed upon me to keep my health condition in control, there were the rules and laws of my household that I had to figure out. The spirit of wonder and ordinary magic was quickly sucked out of my childhood.

I became a grown-up in a child's body.

I went from playing and using my imagination on a daily basis to immersing myself in virtual worlds on-screen. I spent more time ingesting mindless content rather than creating any. I became too lazy to imagine, because these screens were doing the imagining for me.

The development of moving pictures had become progressively more sophisticated in the late 1990s. Large TV boxes suddenly lost tons of weight and became slim monitors. Home phones became cordless, and heavy-duty mobile responders became small, efficient toys with buttons. The complexity of electronics grew exponentially by the year.

At one point, my parents brought a personal desktop computer into our home. The competitive trend between parents at that time was to create tech-savvy children to prepare them for the upcoming technological world. Living in a progressive society, all of us were racing to get an edge over each other. With that commotion, my siblings and I were sent to IT classes to learn about these electronic boxes with complex wires connected to one another.

The gold rush had turned into an *information rush* by the end of the twentieth century.

Time spent being outdoors, immersing myself in books, imagining my animated toys, and connecting with people began to diminish in light of the presence of these virtual screens. I thought it was completely insane that there were other worlds existing inside these monitors. But it was also captivating and fascinating—until fascination gave way to obsession. Everyone started minding their own business, and my need to give and receive personal contact was starved, and slowly forgotten. I fell for that virtual trance as well, and adopted a separation lifestyle of minding my own business.

That was the norm.

Why be connected when there's something much more interesting?

Play and engaging with wonder and ordinary magic were replaced by adventures in a virtual world. It wasn't long before even this was seen as negative in the eyes of parents and teachers. It was a distraction from academics, which was the utmost focus and priority for children of my age. Virtual play became a thing that was frowned upon and needed to be monitored through strict discipline, and both shame and guilt were soon associated with it.

For me, virtual play became a positive reinforcement and incentive to complete my academic priorities. Eventually, even this type of play became a distorted concept, something I had to sneak around and do, remaining hidden from the watchful eyes of adults.

Technological advancement took another leap when I turned ten as we crossed into the new millennium. Predictions that the world was going to end came to nothing. Our human civilization did not collapse due to our own technological advancement. The Y2K bug problem had been managed and was resolved, leading to extraordinarily few technological upsets compared to what had been predicted.

Yet, instead of being an end to our problems, it was the beginning of many. Catching up to the new trends was psychically disorienting. Life sped up extremely fast, and before my emotional maturity was well developed, I was already turning into a young adolescent who was hungry for soulful activities.

That was the time when mass multiplayer online role-playing games (MMORPG) started gaining traction in the masses. I got caught in the wave and played endlessly. I lost track of time and the context of my own reality. I intentionally woke up in the middle of the night just to engage in this play, as if it was my life.

Of course, I did this without my parents knowing.

There was something peculiar about these games. They were offering me something more than I was able to ask for. For a growing child who was enamored with wonder and ordinary magic—and a teenager who was starved of meaningful connection, exploration, and adventure—MMORPG provided solace for me. It fulfilled certain basic psychological needs that were denied and prohibited in my actual reality.

First, it helped me get out of my bodily pain, as I dealt with the rashes and open wounds of the chronic atopic dermatitis. Any escape from that pain was liberating. Besides that, being engaged in MMORPG helped me explore experiences that I otherwise wouldn't be able to have because of the limitations and restrictions imposed by my parents. It gave me a sense of adventure in which I was given safe doses of danger each day, and it enabled me to explore new territories of the virtual world and overcome difficult tasks that I thought were impossible. Moreover, MMORPG provided me with a sense of kinship that I didn't get from my actual world.

I didn't grow up in an environment that prioritized the importance of engaging in meaningful tasks with communal interactions. There was a lot more talking about these ideals as lofty human virtues rather than actually participating in any of them. Worst of all, it seemed normal for people around me to behave in that way.

I noticed that they were living in some sort of trance that they considered to be normal. They called it the "real world." Far from being "real," I was actually living in an environment where we were all disconnected from each other. Being domesticated in city life, we were fearful of nature and stopped seeking out new adventures. The culture of competition and the "dog eat dog" worldview was cultivated, which worsened our emotional capacity to be empathetic on a fundamental level. Our individual development was the utmost priority, and we were acculturated to be competitive with one another. We saw each other more as rivals to be overthrown rather than comrades co-creating harmony and greater success.

Ultimately, we were all struggling with inner conflicts. Deep down we knew that we needed a spirit of collaboration with each other to not just survive but to thrive. Simultaneously, we were all afraid that if we gave too much of ourselves to others, we were going to be cheated, and consequently, we would lose the game of life.

The fabric of society was shaped in such a way that we needed collaboration to succeed, but we were all rewarded individually. Hence, masks of personas were worn, and sinister emotional games were played. The most inconvenient truth was that such a dynamic could be found throughout all levels of society. And it didn't matter whether we were adults or children.

In contrast, within the MMORPG world, the gamers were all perfect strangers, and that kept us safe from any liabilities for being authentically who we were. It gave me a sense of growth and expansion through leveling up and mastering my character. I got a sense of fulfilment and pride out of these tasks, as well as a decent amount of virtual camaraderie because we needed each other to pass certain stages in the game.

Also, engaging in the game became even more fulfilling because I wasn't given a set of rigid rules. I had to figure out the many ways to break through the in-game obstacles. It was addictive because the rate of growth and development in the game was so quick, which provided a dopamine high with a sense of instant gratification.

When I identified myself as a virtual character, I felt immensely powerful and creative. I was able to be witnessed and celebrated for the expression of my creative potential in the virtual world, unlike the real world, where people were only around to criticize and judge. I was completely autonomous and free. And this sense of aliveness encouraged me to escape deeper into the portal of virtual reality.

I found that MMORPG games successfully offered me a chance to craft and explore my personal myth. There was a lot of character development and mythical experiences in the sphere of the game. Upon reflection, such characters were actually a reflection of the creative potential within me. I was fascinated by this connection, and it gave me the idea that perhaps I was able to be more than just a passive participant in the rat race.

Strangely enough, some of the wonder and ordinary magic of life had found a way to seep through the crevices of my blocked consciousness in order to inspire me. The potential to seek the treasure trove of my inner strengths, and taking part of the adventure through the character of the game, was possibly the most joyous nourishment for my soul as a teen. At that point, it only existed in a fictional land of the virtual world, not in actual reality. The problem with this was that the virtual world was nothing more than a parody of real life. I eventually became very bitter, because my actual reality had none of the wonder and ordinary magic that was essential to me.

Neuroses started to become daily occurrences where my mind was swarmed with "if only" thoughts. They were mostly about escaping the pain and suffering of the actual world. I felt completely disoriented from my waking, ordinary life.

I regularly daydreamed about living in a fantasy world where fantastic monsters, beasts, magic, and superhuman strength existed. The bubble of the virtual world eventually burst, and it left me with nothing but utter disappointment, as none of it was close to reality.

Regardless, I still mindlessly engaged in it because it was better than nothing. Games became a mental and spiritual drug that incited my spirit, only to take away my life force in return. It was a short-term solution that had long-term destructive consequences.

And I didn't care.

The longer I prolonged my addictive behavior, the more I felt confined, stuck, disoriented, and mainly confused about the motions of life I was living. I had lost meaningful connections to the world, and I didn't know how to grieve. I felt completely disconnected from society and was stuck in a body that was constantly breaking down.

I was taught to ignore my bodily pains, which numbed me further. It was a detrimental routine—wake up, go to school, take after-school supplementary classes, complete my homework, engage in additional studies, reward myself with some game time, and go to bed, only to repeat the same thing the next weekday.

On weekends, I idled on social media, spoke to friends about how bored we were, hung out mindlessly in shopping malls, and contributed to the capitalistic and materialistic culture. Billboards and advertisements took precedence and bombarded the virtual world. Subsequently, online shopping became the next high. Despite being more connected on the level of technology, I was more disconnected than ever, and it wasn't as if my chronic atopic dermatitis was clearing up, either.

It stuck out like a sore thumb, reminding me that I was broken.

I had forgotten about the wonder and magic in ordinary moments completely, and I replaced it with boredom, which was a sign to look for the next high. The addiction to stimulation after stimulation was rampant. The problem was, I wasn't the only one.

The entire society was built upon virtual, technological activities. We were all warped by being in this unreal portal. Time and space became less obvious. Boundaries became less defined. We, as a collective, had forgotten who we were, what we were here to do, and where we were going.

We were all in a trance of disillusionment.

CHAPTER SEVEN

The Teachings of a
Threshold Guardian

Experiencing plant medicine was a spiraling journey into the depths of my consciousness. I had to confront multiple guardians who were defending the different gates of my consciousness's landscape.

Through the first gate was my waking consciousness. Multiple personas that I had used to identify my sense of self showed up: the son, the scholar, the brother, the dancer, the teacher, the writer, and the student. They were all identities I had taken on. There were even more to be named, and each of them had distinguished voices and opinions about how the world worked and who I was.

Each of my personas told stories in memories, thoughts, images, sound, voices, melodies, vibrations, and tingling body sensations. Visually, auditorily, kinesthetically—the entirety of my bodily instrument spoke stories of the past. It was like sitting in a multidimensional movie where all my senses were stimulated, and the stories were as real as if they had happened right in front of me. I was on the screen, yet I wasn't the person *on* the screen.

Linear time stopped making sense.

The environment of the ceremonial circle started to blur as I continued spiraling down into the unconscious. The space of my body and the environment felt distant. I had jumped right into a dimension where threshold guardians started to look more like mythical, symbolic figures.

Most of them were shadowlike, with no real form. My experience became like a dream, but there was no turning back. The only light available was my loving awareness. Down the portal into my unconsciousness, shadow parts of myself showed up. It was the land of charged-up emotions, many of which were repressed, denied, and rejected. At this point, all I saw were glimpses.

A shapeless guardian eventually showed up and said, "Only the worthy and the ready are allowed through the gate."

This was my chance to be my own hero. No one but me was going to save me. I was no longer the innocent child who played the hero. I was no longer the desperate teen who got lost in the virtual parody of the MMORPG fantasy. Even if this was a psychedelic trip, it was the real deal.

My entire body, soul, and spirit were deeply invested in this journey. I recognized that I was about to go through some trials and tribulations. One of the forces of the Universe would be testing me to see if I was worthy enough to reclaim my own power and my essence, which were lying beneath these tests. It was the moment to decide if I was going to revert to my old comforting yet delusional ways or step into a completely new possibility to reinvent my life.

Keeping in mind my intention and my conviction to remember who I was, I stepped in without hesitation. I had not traveled across the globe into the middle of the forest, and into this otherworldly dimension, just to pull back.

As I stepped through the gate, I was reminded of the story of Siddhartha Gautama, who arrived at his enlightenment while sitting under the Bodhi tree without moving from his seat for forty-nine days. He didn't suddenly achieve enlightenment by just sitting there placidly, though; instead, he had to confront many aspects of himself in the process.

In particular, I thought of Siddhartha's confrontation with Mara, personified as a demon who reflected our human conditioning and egoic temptations. Mara first came with an army, but despite that, Siddhartha did not move an inch. And when that didn't work, Mara then assaulted Siddhartha with weapons of destruction, all of which turned into celestial flowers. Failing again, Mara deployed his daughters of temptations—Desire, Regret, and Lust—to distract Siddhartha from his meditation. Yet it was futile, as Siddhartha remained immovable, with a strong conviction about his quest for truth and enlightenment.

Eventually, after running out of options, Mara challenged Siddhartha for his seat and questioned why he deserved it. Siddhartha did nothing except move his hands to touch the earth gently. And just like that, Earth roared out, "I bear you witness!"

Mara quickly disappeared after that, and the truth of the matter filled up Siddhartha's mind. He was set free with a clarity as bright as a thousand suns. Triumphant over Mara without force but with loving awareness, he was awakened to true seeing, and he finally understood the nature of suffering and broke the chain of causation.

Siddhartha spontaneously transformed into Buddha as he experienced perfect enlightenment. Bathing in that bliss, he continued to sit under the Bodhi tree for another seven days before he set forth to share his teachings that birthed one of the great religions in human history.

That felt like a long haul. But it had to be done.

I saw that the timing of Buddha's story showing up in my mind was no coincidence. It felt like a message from the Grandmother Ayahuasca that such enlightenment was not reserved for Gautama Buddha alone, but a potential that was within each and every sentient being. Buddha was never a person, but a state of enlightenment within all beings.

From one perspective, the trials and tribulations that Buddha faced with Mara felt like an antagonistic interference to our personal heroic journey, and a battle was needed. On the other hand, these trials and tribulations were designed to show me the way back to unity consciousness, which was pure love. Intuitively, I thought that if I could observe my very own Mara with neutrality and equanimity—and more important, with love, compassion, and kindness—only then could such a transformation of consciousness be possible.

As reflected in Gautama Buddha's story, he remained unmoved in the face of Mara, danced the intimate dance of uniting and harmonizing his separated consciousness, and finally attained the ability to see the truth as it was.

And the truth shall set me free. With truth, the love and the light within me shall emanate.

Knowing what lay ahead of me, I was perplexed and torn

within. As much I wanted to be courageous and brave to heal and actualize myself like Siddhartha, I was also experiencing a full-body resistance to moving forward. My body was frozen, and no matter how many blankets I covered myself with, the cold never did subside. The coldness came from within.

Really?

Just one step past the gate and I'm already hesitating?

I thought I had full conviction?

I ended up fighting with myself for a long time while I crossed the gate. It was a battle between lying down, wishing I was able to just fall asleep and forget about all of these nightmares, and sitting up to confront the totality of this experience stemming from the plant medicine. At this point, however, there really was no turning back. It was a bungee jump into the abyss of my shadow world.

So I sat up and focused on catching my breath.

In...and out.

In...and out.

In...and out.

Nothing mattered more than breathing.

As I dived deeper into the shadow world, I was reexperiencing the moments of my life that I thought I had gotten over. There were many memories and emotions that I thought were trivial, yet they were locked away in my unconsciousness. In those moments, I felt apathetic as to why I had to see these things again.

What is the point?

The truth was, I was afraid. It was like the opening of my very own Pandora's Box.

In the Pandora's Box of my consciousness, I found my nemesis, Anger, who had turned into a demonizing monster because she had been oppressed, locked up in a cage, and not given the place and space to speak her truth. She was raging at many things in life: at the people who overstepped my boundaries; at those who took advantage of my kindness; at the authorities who had taken my voice away; at the circumstances of my illness, which had taken my freedom away; at the failures and rejection of my creative expression; and at God, Who had put me into such a difficult existence without proper guidance.

Anger blamed my incompetent skills for mismanaging my own life. She didn't want to be the victim. The act of blaming somehow felt empowering for her. It was easier when there was a scapegoat to point the finger at. All this blaming was done to avoid pain.

The truth of the matter was that I was hurt.

The coldness that I experienced was actually the numbness that I had habitually accumulated over the years of my life. It was there to protect me from my hurt.

Perhaps if I directed my attention to an outside source and not turn within, then I didn't have to feel the pain. As tempting as it was to blame outer circumstances for my unhappiness, deep down I knew that I was actually angry at myself for not being able to make the changes I wanted to see in my life.

I was completely helpless when I developed chronic atopic dermatitis.

I was angry for being powerless and having the lack of courage to assert my life in the way I wanted to.

I was angry that I got into those situations of anguish and despair as a result of my own incompetence in managing life's situations and my emotional reactions.

This truth was hard to hear, and I was startled by how wise Anger was.

The personification of Anger had a ghastly appearance, which later shape-shifted into round-shaped worms that looked like ancient millipedes. There were two of them forming a circular shape and rotating side by side, forming fractals of sacred geometry.

I was traveling into the core of the vortex endlessly. I was diving into a dark portal of darkness, into a black hole of my consciousness. With my head pounding heavily in protest, the base of my lower back to the tail of my spinal cord started to buzz violently, as if I were growing a tail.

Images of cats of different sizes and shapes started to emerge in my vision. My body, with a mind of its own, started to be enveloped by catlike behavior. The heat in my body increased, and I started sweating profusely despite the cold night. At some point, I felt the inner coldness that I had felt earlier subside, and it was as if the cold walls protecting my heart were slowly melting.

My instincts were reawakened, and the basic primal desires of hunting, feeding, playing, socializing, and procreating started to overtake my human rationale. Yawning became involuntary, but it wasn't out of exhaustion, but a feeling that my jaw bones were reshaping, extending outward, and needing more space for new teeth to grow. I started clenching my teeth and felt the desire to bite and gnaw. I was turning into a nocturnal predatorial beast as I underwent these changes.

I was shape-shifting with Anger, as she was reintegrating her energy into me. She was "rewilding" herself into my being. Right away, my animal nature returned, and the connection to establish a new relationship contract with my human nature was initiated. I felt that I had reclaimed a lost part of my self, which was essential to my larger journey to live my authentic, true nature.

Yet, Anger was not done with me.

She didn't wish to perpetuate unhealthy expressions, so she had more messages to pass on.

I understood that the crumbling of my life's happiness was nature's foolproof way of showing where and how I was ignorant and in denial. It was a wake-up call to initiate a process of awakening that was able to realign me with the deeper truths of my being.

I had always known.

I was just selectively and willfully looking in another direction.

Turning a blind eye was easier and less painful.

I understood that the circumstances of my health, my relationships, and my freedom were just reflections of how I valued myself and what I believed about myself and the world. After all, my human limitations had never allowed me to perceive the complete truth, but only subjective truths through the filter of my rose-colored beliefs.

Pain, symptoms, toxic relationships, emotional stress, and self-sabotaging behaviors were all catalytic portals or transformational gateways to show me the next evolution of my true nature. What that meant was that I had to surrender my limiting beliefs and false expectations of how my life was supposed to turn out, who I thought I was, and what this world was meant to be. In doing so, only then would my innate intelligence be able to take me all the way to the original nature of my soul that all along had been emanating love, light, and truth.

That destination seemed far-fetched, as I knew how willful, righteous, and attached I was to my own ideas and philosophy about life. None of what I thought was right actually mattered. I was resistant to such an understanding because it felt too simple to be true.

I was afraid that if I completely surrendered myself, I would lose control, and eventually the life that I knew would stop existing. Agonizingly, such resistance created more pain.

When the shape-shifting stopped, I entered a different dimension of experience—one of unconditional bliss and wakefulness. I felt like a diamond: pristine and clear. Truth had multiple layers, which made me wonder how many layers I still had to go through to reach the eternal, permanent truth.

Truth spoke:

"It wasn't your fault and your fault alone. Neither was it the fault of others. Nor was it the fault of Anger. They were all circumstances that were caused by your reactive behavior that had been conditioned by past circumstances—individual, genetic, environmental, intergenerational past lives, many more.

"So, forgive yourself to forgive others; forgive the reactive nature of your circumstances that you weren't able to identify, to see, to feel because of your limited consciousness.

"You weren't broken, and neither was the world.

"Only your perspective of the world was broken.

"You were brought here to be more aware of the infinite possible ways to love and be compassionate. What happened in the past was not your fault, but what you do from here on in is fully your responsibility. You are here to be 'response-able' skillfully through love, so show and lead others the way.

"Do not worry how you will get there; just focus on your heart's deepest desire.

"Your heart knows the next best step.

"Follow the longing.

"Follow the bliss!"

The message only lasted momentarily, but it was serene and clear. Delving into the most profound point of darkness was where the immensity of pure light emanated.

Perhaps that was enlightenment, and a glimpse of what being a *Homo luminous* felt like.

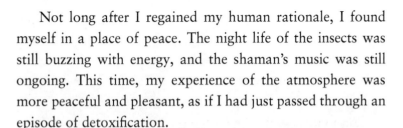

Not long after I regained my human rationale, I found myself in a place of peace. The night life of the insects was still buzzing with energy, and the shaman's music was still ongoing. This time, my experience of the atmosphere was more peaceful and pleasant, as if I had just passed through an episode of detoxification.

The process of forgetfulness into remembrance was a refreshing feeling. I felt a sense of completion and integration where I sat in a lotus pose, fully relaxed with each bone of my spine stacked perfectly on top of the another. I had a strong back, a soft front, and a wild heart that was fully alive.

Despite the difficulty and pain of this remembrance, re-experiencing these moments eventually took me to a place of liberation, a feeling of lightness in my body, and a grounding experience of love and gratitude.

I was taught by Grandmother Ayahuasca that only when we experience the moments of our life fully could emotions—the energy-in-motion or our life force—be able to assimilate and flow through our bodily systems. When we experience our life fully without the constraints of the judgmental mind, that is when creative-expression channels for the emotions of the moment are able to emerge.

Emotions have their own intelligence of creative expression, and we need to learn to befriend them. When emotions are allowed for authentic expression, their natural intelligence flows in the path of least resistance. And that path of least resistance is the natural flow of the Universe.

Instead of creating rupture and destruction, the creative energy of our emotions is designed to create a loving and compassionate outcome. I had to relearn to trust the instinctual, primal nature of my emotions. I had to harmonize both my animal instincts and my human intellect to become whole. The lesson was about synchronizing my soul, mind, emotions, and body so that they worked as one, rather than in conflict with one another.

When all these faculties came into alignment, I felt my connection to the Great Spirit. I felt the presence of all sentience, elements, and energy around me. And in this connection came equilibrium and flow.

In that timeless experience, I learned that the Universe is

a living intelligence that directs every independent action interconnectedly toward the cosmic flow where wonder and ordinary magic occur.

This is what it truly meant to know the magnitude of the Divine Grace of the Universe. By flowing with the Universe, I learned to become an active participant of life and what authenticity meant for me. In being an active participant, I became what I had been looking for.

CHAPTER EIGHT
The Gift of Forgetfulness

Every plant-medicine ayahuasca ceremony was followed by an integration circle where we shared our experiences to learn from each participant. It was an intentional space to harvest the wisdom of the collective.

Entering one ceremony after another, like peeling the layers of an onion, I felt the veil of misperception become thinner. I found that there was a collective theme in each ceremony, and within that, our personal themes connected and integrated ingeniously. Another person's sharing became everyone's learning experience. This reflection helped me understand that the fundamental nature of our consciousness is inherently interconnected. We're never quite separated despite what our perceptions have led us to believe.

After completing the one-month retreat with Paititi, the experience of being in proximity with nature gave birth to a great ambition in me. Nature's intelligence had left me with a feeling of awe, which inspired me to further discover the principles of nature and how to live my human life according to natural law. Many of these principles were untold and un-integrated in our modern society. I wanted to decipher them and share them with the world, to begin a long-awaited conversation among humans.

I thought that if our modern world was going to have the possibility of creating an enlightened society, then we need-ed to remember and integrate these natural principles in our daily living. To begin, I knew I had to start with me. It would have been a shame to remember nature's sacred code of living harmoniously, and then just forget this truth when I returned to city life.

Partaking in a plant-medicine ayahuasca ceremony didn't assure me of any form of enlightenment. What it did give me, though, was a brief dialogue with the depths of my conscious-ness, as well as a precious moment to be in direct connection with nature and the Divine Grace of the Universe.

This experience helped the seed of the Homo luminous within me to sprout. What was left for me was to continue nurturing that seed with wisdom, compassion, and courage. For me, that looked like radically accepting and loving my-self while revering every single moment of my life; appreci-ating the joy of simple pleasures; and following the calling of my inner purpose to express my entelechy every single day. Sprouting the seed of *Homo luminous* also meant seeing with awe and wonder that every single manifestation of life came from the same source. I had to learn how to revere all of life— all of its moments—and all sentient beings equally with love and respect.

Yet, despite this profound level of understanding, I knew that there would come a moment in the future when I would forget what I had learned from Grandmother Ayahuasca. For me to embrace the heart-opening psychedelic experience fully, I had to be earnest about my human conditioning of forgetfulness. I knew that if I left it unchecked, it had the potential to deteriorate into numbness. And if I was too stubborn and dishonest to make any changes, that numbness would eventually turn into spiritual arrogance, which stems from ignorance and apathy.

So many of us are influenced by the pop-the-pill culture, so I knew that we're often too quick to numb our emotional pain or mask the symptoms of our bodies without listening to them closely. As a collective, we habitually cope by distracting our attention from the truth of the matter, and we easily fall for the cheap and quick solution of temporary relief. Little do we know that our pain, fear, and stress serve as feedback and information about the conditions of the environment we live in.

For example, when a plant grows unhealthily, it isn't the plant that we need to fix; it's the soil and the conditions that the plant is living in. Similarly, it isn't the emotional pain or the symptoms of our body that we need to fix; it's the conditions of our environment that created that distress in the first place.

To work with forgetfulness, I learned that I had to first and foremost continually embrace, support, and understand my hypersensitivity. It was because I didn't understand how to work with it that had led me to repress Anger in the first place, allowing it to mutate into an inner demon that I was afraid of owning.

To avoid repeating the past, I had to learn how to befriend the full spectrum of my human emotions; unlearn all my unhealthy ways of coping with overwhelming situations; and develop a healthy relationship with pain, fear, and stress. I realized that I had to give myself the daily reminder to slow down my life rather than speed it up. I felt that I could do so by practicing turning within, which meant pausing my mental activity and intentionally connecting to my bodily senses. I learned that taking a long, deep breath was the most effective way to do so.

From the practices I learned during my time with Paititi, I learned how to drop into the mind space of loving awareness at will. Previously, it had just been a concept that I had learned from my Buddhist teachers and meditation classes. Fortunately, I had gotten a glimpse of it in Encinitas while I was trying to resolve my existential angst. And as a result of this psychedelic experience, I had an opportunity to have a direct experience with it, making loving awareness an integral part of me.

When observing life from this perspective, I knew that no matter what happened on the outside, nothing was able to take away my inner peace and freedom. I had learned that *awareness is medicine*, and I wondered if loving awareness was an important clue to healing my lifelong battle with chronic atopic dermatitis. Regardless, I knew that staying connected with loving awareness would keep my human senses awakened, ensuring that the rapture of being fully alive would never be forgotten.

Being fully alive, free, and fulfilled had nothing to do with chasing after any dreams; instead, I needed to be fully present in the moment, *living* the dream. The dream was never somewhere *out there*, but right here in front of me all along. To never forget meant to live purposefully and intentionally rather than reactively, even if I had to go against the grain. As such,

I had to be courageous and make sure that I didn't succumb to an easy way out embodied in conformity.

I learned that powerful experiences require an intentional period for integration, meaning that whatever I learned had to be practiced, and implemented into my day-to-day life, to form new habits. Along with these new habits, a new embodiment of self-expression could be created. And with this new embodiment of self-expression, a new identity could be born. This process was important because with my newfound identity, I could create a new paradigm of life that was so loving and powerful that it would make my previous fears and limiting ways obsolete. Success in doing so meant that I could fully transform my life.

Insights that I had gained from my transformational epiphany, when not acted upon, would become just another beautiful experience. The consequence of that meant going back to square one, where my old, self-sabotaging habits would dominate my life once again. If that was the case, then it would be as if I had not started to change at all.

Transformational change is like a software update for programming consciousness: just like computers, we require some time for installation. However, once installed, the installation cannot be undone. I wouldn't be able to unknow what I already knew.

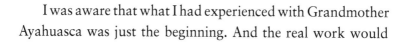

I was aware that what I had experienced with Grandmother Ayahuasca was just the beginning. And the real work would only begin after I left the mountain. I was honest about the fallacies of my own conditioning to create the long-term sustainable change I desired. I wondered if my friends and family would understand what I'd been through and be able to accept my new changes.

Will they continue to accept me?

Will I succumb to the addiction of the virtual world again?

Or will I have the courage to stay true to my own wonder and ordinary magic?

Will I lose my soul?

Or will I stay true to being ordinarily me?

There were so many distractions and temptations waiting for me in city life. There were so many comforts in the city that were able to numb my soul. And there were so many expectations from others about who I was supposed to be.

What will I do in the face of these pressures?

This made me feel that forgetfulness was inevitable, but nothing was hopeless.

After all, the process of remembrance requires the counterpart of forgetfulness. Becoming *Homo luminous* is only possible if there is dullness in one's consciousness. Courage is only discovered in the presence of fear. Evolution, maturation, and transformation are only initiated if there are problems, conflicts, issues, traumas, suffering, and so on. The paradox is that forgetfulness is just as enlightening as remembrance. I realized that coming into unconditional acceptance of life as it is and continuously expanding my loving awareness was the key to the transformational process.

No one is intended to stay enlightened all the time. The more we're attached to remembrance, the more it is likely that we will get lost in it and end up in forgetfulness. Yet, the more we embrace the natural process of forgetfulness through humor and compassion, the more we're inclined to engage in remembrance. This is a function of being on the path of equanimity.

Equanimity is about embracing the imperfect quality of our human nature. It exists so that there are spaces and opportunities to practice the art of perfection within our imperfection. Only within imperfections can the evolution of life begin.

The famous logo of the Apple corporation mirrors this concept. The logo looks like it has been bitten off on purpose, which means that their business was never meant to be complete or perfected, but rather, constantly growing and expanding through adversities and imperfections. As such, the creation of a never-ending flow of activity is possible.

When anything is connected to the principle of universal flow, abundance follows, just like in nature. This is true for us humans as well. When we surrender and truly accept all of our conditioning without resistance, life becomes easy, like we're flowing down a river.

I once heard singer Jason Mraz, in his live version of "I Never Knew You," ask, "What is it about humanness that we remember and forget?"

And he answered, "I think it is an opportunity of enlightenment. So that we can be awakened again and again and again. Because it feels good to remember our greatness."

I completely agree with him.

Forgetfulness reminds us of our attachment to enlightened experiences—our perpetual chase for meaning and enlightened experiences that have stopped us from truly experiencing our very own expression of *Homo luminous*. And that very feedback, in return, allows us to remember an opportunity—

that we're always one with life, never separated, and already enlightened to begin with.

Each remembrance becomes an opportunity to drop into loving awareness, and within that space is the opportunity to deepen our appreciation and gratitude for our human experience. We're reminded that our humanness is undeniably healthy, whole, and complete to begin with. Therefore, we were never meant or made to seek the meaning of life, but rather, to follow our bliss by creating opportunities to experience the rapture of being fully alive and being completely immersed in wonder and ordinary magic. The gift of forgetfulness then becomes a precious gem in our human experience to remind us of that, and it is the very doorway toward the Divine Grace of the Universe.

As I wrote after completing the arduous journey of diving deep into plant medicine in the middle of the Peruvian jungle:

Wonder and magic are part of our everyday existence. Thus, they are very ordinary, indeed. It isn't a matter of whether magic exists or not, but a matter of perception and attunement. Attunement has to do with a deep connection to the fundamental basis of reality.

Many modern humans have switched off this capacity. Not only do we chronically disconnect from this ordinary magic, but we also put up a lot of resistance to rejuvenate this capacity. We do everything we can do to protect our safely molded version of reality, as the totality of reality is such a powerful force that it can shake the fundamental structure of our molded reality.

We will not know what to do with this newfound truth.

Nevertheless, magic has never really left our consciousness.

We unconsciously create it in our movies, our music, and our art as we call out for that deep yearning to return to this sacred, magical connection within the womb of the Universe.

We end up creating a delusional form of romantic magic —something far-fetched, unrealistic, and ungrounded. It becomes a parody. This romanticism colors our vision and is devoid of any clarity as far as what is real and what is not. This sends us into a downward spiral of our delusions, as we become chronically disconnected.

The answer is for us to empty our cups; clean our dusty, rose-colored glasses; and return simply to our ordinariness. Without expectations about what life should or should not be and what magic is and is not, we can return to be in alignment and reconnection with the ordinary magic that we fundamentally understand to be our true nature. Only in moments such as these does the Divine Grace of the Universe show Herself.

When we recognize our inner wonder and ordinary magic, and appreciate our existence from that standpoint, then ordinary magic will start playing out through our external lives. We will become witches, wizards, and alchemists of our world to co-create magic with the Great Spirit of Life.

With this, I took my month-long training in the mountains back with me into city life. I vowed to continue to sow the seeds of wonder and ordinary magic, and I made every effort to remember what I'd learned from Grandmother Ayahuasca so that the Divine Grace of the Universe could enter my life.

Despite my efforts, and as expected, forgetfulness was set in motion. Before I knew it, I was slipping back into old habits while chronic atopic dermatitis continued to run rampant through my life. But this time, at least I knew that this disease was not my enemy, but rather, a precious friend from the sub-conscious desiring to protect me and set me free.

So I continued to ponder, *What else am I missing in order for me to heal?*

What do I need to do to finally come home to my very own expression of Homo luminous?

PART THREE

Connection: The Courage to Be Vulnerably Openhearted

"I believe we are the greatest technology expressed by nature so far. And so, what's our technological journey ultimately? To supercharge our five senses into seeing the full beauty of this planet, so that everything will change—the very matrix by which we live, breathe, think and imagine within—is here to shift in this moment. If we really see the universe for its beauty, it will switch completely. Every atom will change."

—Dr. Zach Bush, from the *Rich Roll* podcast, Ep. 751

CHAPTER NINE

Nature's Law of Love and Respect

I t was the middle of the night, and only the luminous river of stars lit up the land. The constellations of stars in the Southern Hemisphere were a lot different from what I was used to. Being a seasoned stargazer from the Northern Hemisphere, I found the night sky in the south very disorienting.

The only constellation I knew was the Southern Cross, and I wasn't able to track the usual zodiacs that I knew about. As such, the night sky in South Africa felt a little emptier, which made the air heavier, with the presence of solitude. The quieter the night, the wider the field of such a presence, which seemed to have stopped time.

I appreciated the rare moment of being both outdoors and awake at this hour. It helped me feel a little closer to nature, which created a more intimate connection with myself. It was a perfect setting for contemplation, and perhaps a good time to have another self-illuminating conversation with the Universe.

It had been a long, quiet night—I knew I wouldn't be able to easily fall asleep in this new time zone. Combined with my excitement about my next adventure, the heat in my room made it even more difficult for me to feel fully relaxed. The odd thing was that the more I tried to fall asleep, the more impossible it was. Feeling restless and noticing the futility of sleeping, I decided to go outside and get some fresh, cool air.

After traveling over three continents for a day and a half, I thought it was surreal to actually be here in Timbavati, the native land where the mysterious white lions first appeared. Previously considered a freak of nature, speculated as an albino species, and falsely assumed to have weaker camouflage and hunting abilities, the white lions are actually the subspecies of Panthera leo that uniquely held significant cultural, spiritual, and ecological conservation roles.

Now here I was in the heartlands where the white lions roamed. I wondered what new mysteries awaited me and why the Universe had called me to visit this place.

I had flown from Denver to Boston to London to Johannesburg and finally arrived at Hoedspruit Airport, which was located within the UNESCO Kruger-to-Canyons Biosphere that was also the home to a concentrated biodiversity of wildlife. The reality of being physically present here finally hit me after spending weeks thinking about this trip.

When I got off the plane, I felt as lost as a stray animal. Even the monkeys that were busy assaulting the trash cans by the corner of the airport seemed more at home than I was.

The bushveld wasn't what I expected. Everything felt like death and decay around the airport, and the conditions of the land contradicted the image in mind of African safaris, which I used to see depicted in *National Geographic* or on the Discovery channel.

Before departing on this trip, I had done my own my research on Timbavati. I discovered that it was one of the most popular game reserves in South Africa. However, behind the well-established reserves was an inexplicable darkness where wildlife was exploited for human entertainment and business profit.

I was puzzled, and my head was filled with questions.

Right away, I noticed the diversity of people gathered at the small airport and the number of shuttles that were parked outside. That was a clue that Timbavati was likely an international hot spot for tourism.

As I was making my way into the arrival hall, I told myself that this wasn't the time to get lost in delving into the big questions of life. I had a more immediate concern to worry about—my luggage—which had gone through the same number of transits that I had just to get here. I was particularly wary about its location, because luggage from my previous long-flight journeys had disappeared before.

No matter how much I prepared, unexpected situations were sure to arise. As much as I love new adventures in unfamiliar, remote places, the control freak within is just as afraid of uncertainty. I've had to learn to trust my innate instincts to make spontaneous decisions if anything happened.

I eventually found my luggage, and my anxiety subsequently settled down. Everything seemed to move forward very smoothly and according to plan, as the staff member who was supposed to pick me up found me effortlessly. Very quickly, we were making our way to the Tsau! Conservancy, where the Global White Lion Protection Trust was.

And here I was, struggling on my first night to get some decent sleep.

Perhaps the anxious energy I had felt earlier at the airport had not actually subsided yet.

Why did the bushveld around the airport not seem quite alive?

Furthermore, why did most of the land on the way to Tsau! Conservancy feel like it was deteriorating?

I didn't come this far for a vacation. In fact, traveling had not been a vacation since I had set my heart on a quest for healing and to actualize the greater purpose of my life. These travels were intentional, but they were also aimless saunters that provided me alone time to tune out the white noise of others. As such, I was able to drop into the space of loving awareness, tune in to the voice of my heart, and listen for clues from the Universe.

Being here at the heartlands of the white lions felt like I was approaching another pertinent clue toward healing and coming home to my entelechy. Being born in the astrological sign of Leo, I felt a strong affinity for the regal and sovereign presence of a lion. I wanted to know how I would be able to rise up to become a leader that matched such a spirit.

However, what sealed the deal for me to come all the way here was a story I'd heard about a courageous woman who had a powerful initiation in nature. She had confronted a near-death experience when she and her friends were encircled by a pride of angry lions right here in the African bushveld itself. Miraculously, they were saved by a Shangaan shaman who later played an important role in leading her on a nearly impossible mission of protecting the white lions.

The woman's name was Linda Tucker, and she had founded the Global White Lion Protection Trust to protect and reintroduce white lions back into their endemic lands of Timbavati where they had become extinct owing to the exploitative practices of trophy hunting, extraction, and illegal trade. She had also created the Academy for LionHearted Leadership, which I signed up to participate in for a month. I had come here with a mission for myself—to be trained as a leader who could become a powerful change agent who served both the natural and human worlds, just as Linda did.

I remembered when I first picked up *Mystery of the White Lions*, a book written by Linda that was imbued with mysteries of the past, the magic of nature, and a concern for humanity's enlightenment. As soon as I got my hands on it, I wasn't able to stop flipping the pages—Linda's words stirred my soul, which had been in slumber, and that immediate soul connection helped me finish the book in one day.

Furthermore, throughout the book, Linda had pinpointed the reason why I had always been so deeply connected to the bright, luminous blue star Sirius. Africa's greatest knowledge keeper, Credo Mutwa, had shared the original meaning of the name Timbavati with Linda. It means "the place where the StarLions came down" and according to legend, the white lions had descended from Sirius. Both mythical and literal, the white lions are the Starlions.

It was a story that felt so familiar to my heart, and there was an ineffable knowing that every word had been written with love and truth. While reading about the mysteries of the white lions, that wonder and ordinary magic that I had not felt since my time with Grandmother Ayahuasca was stirred up within me once again.

Perhaps it was fiction; perhaps it was real. It didn't matter. The calling from the Universe was genuine, and the tug toward having a direct experience with these divine beings was telling. All that mattered was that my heart knew—and after all, truth was self-evident and needed no proof. This deep connection was enough for me to travel many miles from home to experience the living myth of these majestic white lions. I knew I was on a monumental trip that would be a once-in-a-lifetime experience.

What luck to actually be here!

Only a year after my pivotal journey in Peru with Grandmother Ayahuasca, here I was, stepping into another. A universal force larger than myself was moving me again.

Meeting Linda for the first time was like meeting a lioness in human form. Her presence was regal and noble, and she had a unique way of communicating the teachings of the white lions. Every time she spoke, the air got denser, her words carrying the weight that grounded all nine of us students to listen to her attentively. She ignited our hearts easily, and her storytelling made difficult and heavy topics of the world's crises easier to grasp. She also embodied a powerful maternal energy that made us feel like exploring parts of ourselves that we had difficulty facing. Her enlightening wisdom sparked courage and instilled hope in all of us, which made it natural for us to take spontaneous and inspired action.

Linda had the qualities of leadership that I hoped to emulate: a strong back, a soft front, and a wild heart. Moreover, she had the seriousness of a reliable adult and the innocence of a child who was connected to her very own sense of wonder and ordinary magic.

It was very moving to know that powerful yet gentle leaders like Linda existed. Her daily operating system was all about moving and leaning in the direction of fear, conflict, and destruction with absolute love, trust, and faith. As part of that process, she developed the power and wisdom to turn what was considered impossible into the possible.

She had the force of nature on her side.

Why?

How does she embody the force of nature that is able to move mountains, heal the seemingly unhealable, and transform the deepest crevices of humanity's darkness?

Every time I met someone with such qualities, I knew one thing for sure: They had gone through overwhelming trials and tribulations that had tested their wits, their will, and their woes. They had to rise above their own ignorance, which opened them up to great wisdom that was within their wits. Through confronting their fears and aversions, they had given birth to the great courage that was within their will. And last, the trials and tribulations of the Universe had taught them difficult lessons related to surrendering their attachments, only to show them the great compassion that was present within their woes all along.

It all boiled down to one word: *humility.* Humility was all about openheartedness, which opened the doorway to love and respect for all of life, causing the ego to make space so that the Divine Grace of the Universe could move *through* us and as us. Humility also meant *"ubuntu,"* which simply translated to "common humanity." Or even better, this old African philosophy was translated as "I am because we are." Humility allowed for true love and respect to be expressed by seeing people as living sentient beings, as the embodiment of sacred intelligence to be revered, and not as resources or commodities. Within that worldview came great influence and the power to make profound changes to create the beautiful world we knew to be possible. As such, humility had the capacity to transform our egocentric intentions into *ecocentric* ones.

From an ecocentric perspective, the main intention is to fully embrace and appreciate Mother Nature in everything we do. This means conducting our daily lives with a mindset that takes into consideration the entire ecosystem. With this mindset, we form a personal identity that recognizes nature as a fundamental aspect of our being. This identity is also known as our *ecological self*, a concept introduced by Norwegian philosopher Arne Næss.

Through Linda's stories, I was able to see that she accepted her calling wholeheartedly, showing up relentlessly to her life's purpose, which was revealed to her as she walked her journey. In surrendering her life to the Universe with humility, her loving presence became a force of nature in the world that reverberated through the hearts of all beings.

"What about my destiny?" I asked the Universe, eager for answers.

I waited for a response, but this time, it was completely silent.

However, I did hear the distant roar of a lion echoing

through the darkness of the night. Unlike the fearsome roars heard in movies, those that I was hearing now sounded more like rhythmical, low-pitched echoes of grunting.

This was the famous, lengthy "back roar" of a lion that I had heard about before coming here. Strangely, rather than fearing what might lurk out there in the darkness, I felt blessed by the lions' presence. As I quieted my mind to listen to the sounds, I felt a certain comfort, as if these divine beings were acknowledging that I was where I needed to be.

"Kairos," I whispered, acknowledging the serendipity and synchronicity that led me to be here. I didn't know why, I didn't know how, but in that moment, I felt a sense of belonging, of finally coming home.

▓▓
▓▓

The many days of our training at the academy focused on discussing the cultural, spiritual, and ecological significance of the white lions; learning some foundations of animal communication; and paying many visits to the nearby pride. The routine started with waking up before daylight each day to practice breathwork and meditation so we could tune in to our hearts. After that, we went to visit the pride, always making sure that we didn't interrupt their routines.

We were taught to show love and respect, yet it was important for us to come from the perspective of nature rather than from our own egocentric or humancentric version of what love and respect was. For example, we learned to look at these divine beings with a soft gaze and communicate with them by blinking slowly, just as we might with any feline, such as a pet cat.

We were also taught not to behave like prey by freaking out or standing up in the open-air truck, as those behaviors frequently stirred and aggravated the lions' powerful and predatory instincts. If anything were to happen, we were given instructions to relax and be still.

We did not intrude on the lions and instead watched them from a respectful distance, unless they decided to grace us with their presence by coming to us. Sometimes we weren't able to see them at all. This wasn't out of chance but out of their choice. I believed the white lions always knew we were looking for them miles before we arrived at a serendipitous meeting point to catch their presence. They knew where to meet us halfway.

But did we?

When I encountered them for the first time, I knew that they were definitely no ordinary animals, but rather, emanations of spiritual perfection within animal bodies that radiated so much love and light. Only stubborn and ignorant fools who weren't connected to their gut instincts or spiritual senses would dare to challenge them.

When we were making our rounds through the heartlands of the white lions, we were all mostly silent, which gave me the opportunity to turn within to have a private conversation with myself. I spent most of my time contemplating my connection with nature while observing what was in front of me.

There was an incident that took place near the borders of the heartlands, which I haven't been able to get off my mind. The borders were fenced off with the purpose of sealing off threats from the poachers. I saw that on one side, any land that was touched by the white lions' paws and graced by their presence was thriving. In contrast, at the other side of the fence, where trophy hunting and commoditization of wildlife was taking place, the land was desolate and barren. It finally made complete sense why I'd felt so much anxiety at the airport when I first arrived. There was an energetic dissonance that was emanating out of the land rather than the usual energetic coherence that I was familiar with when I stepped into proximity with nature. It was a heartbreaking yet inspiring scene to experience as a microcosm mirroring the current global state of affairs.

This phenomenon reminded me of the desolation of Pride Rock in Disney's *The Lion King*, when the noble leader wasn't present in his homeland. However, when Simba emerged victorious from his challenge with Scar, the entire ecosystem surrounding Pride Rock recovered on its own. I used to think that such a thing could only happen in animated films or our imaginations.

However, this understanding changed when my research on healing led me to the story of wolves that had restored an entire ecosystem when they were reintroduced to their natural habitat at Yellowstone National Park in the United States. This healing phenomenon was called *trophic cascading*, and it was a natural ecological event. The reintroduction of the apex predators or keystone species to their natural habitats led to a thriving ecological change in the ecosystem where barren land was able to regenerate and literally come back to life. Nature had always been resilient, and it was made to thrive when the right conditions were met. Just like with the teachings of the white lions, it all came back to the law of love and respect.

Learning that such potency was dormant within all of us rekindled the flame of hope within my heart, as I knew I was living in a time of humanity's greatest destruction. I learned that by restoring our hearts with the spirit of the white lions, and by realigning our behavior and interaction with nature and with each other accordingly, this naturally reflected the law of love and respect.

Being ethical, kind, and loving, then, was a no-brainer.

I saw how it was possible to turn the tides of our greatest destruction into a golden opportunity to co-create a beautiful world. Innately, we were able to transform the world, just like the apex predators of Yellowstone and also here in Timbavati. We had forgotten that nature wasn't just all around us but within us. The force of nature lives within us all, but only a few embody it.

The forces of nature are so beautiful. Contrary to the common belief that prey are the victims and made to be dominated by the predators, I discovered that the hunt between the prey and the predator is actually a life-affirming dance. By surrendering their flesh to the predator, prey animals gift their bodies and spirits to the ascending spiral of life.

There is a story about a white lion who was too injured to hunt and close to dying of starvation. Because it was not in divine timing for the lion to ascend to the spiritual realm, a wildebeest presented its flesh as an offering.

Why would any being in its right mind sacrifice itself? That wildebeest must be crazy!

But it is only insane if we look at nature from our human-centric eyes.

How often are we able to see life from the eyes of nature or our ecological self?

Through this story, I realized that life happens because there is death. Life does not sustain life. Death does. All phenomena in nature exist to sustain and to evolve life. By gifting itself through the process of true predation, the wildebeest was integrated into the white lion so that its spirit played a role in the white lion's governance of the land, allowing all life to thrive.

As told by Linda, this dance of nature was represented by a vivid picture in her dreams of a spiral rotation of a mountainous tower where wildebeests were running toward the top to meet the apex predators. Symbolically, this dream shared that the wildebeests and the lions were all one to begin with, interacting in a sacred relationship for the evolution of life.

Learning about this story forever changed my perception, and it got me thinking, *How do I bring nature's law of love and respect to our human world and my own relationships?*

Life is full of polarity in our human world, filled with volatile, uncertain, complex, and ambiguous problems. Growing up, I felt that everyone always considered themselves to be right. I believed that everyone was acting out of their best interests. We were all doing our best as much as we knew how, and we were making choices based on what we believed was best.

But was our best creating a harmonious world?

I don't think so!

Modern humans behave with arrogance and a strong sense of entitlement. Any argument is able to be made sensible even if, deep down in our humble hearts, we know we are in misalignment. We are all deeply attached to our own tunnel vision of self-righteousness that is our autopilot mode.

Maybe that is the problem.

We're living too much in our heads and very little in our hearts.

We're seeing the brokenness of the world through our broken minds and have little awareness of the defective perception of our minds that we cling to so strongly. This leads us to make unloving choices that don't match the energetic coherence of our hearts.

A powerful mind without a heart is blind and destructive.

A passionate heart without a mind is ineffective.

This is why in Tibetan Buddhism, both wisdom and compassion have to be present in order to develop impactful, skillful means. Volatile, uncertain, complex, and ambiguous problems of our world can never be solved through a preexisting paradigm. Just like architect/philosopher Buckminster Fuller once brilliantly advised: "You never change things by fighting the existing reality. To change something, build a new model that makes the existing model obsolete." Solutions and answers to our problems have to be fresh, spontaneous, and alive in the moment. And to add another component to that equation, I believe that courage has to be present, along with wisdom and compassion. Otherwise, no outcome can come to fruition, as no action is taken.

And I kept wondering, *What actually happens when the heart and the mind form a bridge?*

What actually happens when we fully trust our gut feelings and act upon them?

Is it possible for the heart to have a love affair with the mind so strong that in their union, our health is spontaneously restored, our relationships naturally thrive, and complex problems become as simple as one, two, three?

Are we able to create trophic cascading in the health of our body and in the relationships of our lives, just like the wolves and the white lions?

I felt that no fanciful ideas or any sophisticated philosophy would be able to answer these questions. As such, I intuitively reflected that only through a radical paradigm shift of seeing through the eyes of nature's law of love and respect would I be able to receive an illuminating answer.

CHAPTER TEN

Dysfunctional Love Operating System

A couple of weeks into the program at Timbavati, I noticed that my mind stopped racing. Falling asleep was easier, and waking up in the morning was something I looked forward to. Regardless, it wasn't always fun and games. There were moments that challenged us as a group and as individuals, but within those challenges were opportunities to transform our self-centeredness.

Our city-dwelling habits that seemed to be hardwired in our system were still playing out, even in the wild. There were moments when we weren't able to get along, for instance. But despite our differences, our daily visits when we were in communion with the white lions were something our hearts were able to come together for. They were precious moments.

I started to see that we didn't have to like each other to love one another's humanity. Just like the lions, when they didn't like something, they gave clear feedback and communicated transparently, but never kept their conflicts locked within their hearts.

I thought the relationship between the "Royal Trinity" to be the most intriguing of them all. This was a trio of two females, Zihra and Nebu, who were a mother-daughter pair, and a male who used to be an outsider but seemed to have developed a deep bond with the other two. His name was Assegaia, which resonated deeply within my heart.

Assegaia means "the shield of stars that protects Mother Earth." Shy, protective, and gentle, he had this quiet presence of fierce love that mirrored qualities that I knew I had within me. It was intriguing to watch him interact with the others, and I was determined to find a connection with him through the animal communication skills that I had learned. Assegaia was exactly the kind of leader I wanted to emulate in the world.

The story behind the trio was that they had not always gotten along. Nebu had a fierce reputation for making uncompromising boundaries, especially after her father (and the previous ruler of the land), Mandla, had passed to the spiritual realm. From the stories that were told, Nebu was testing Assegaia's integrity, making sure that he deserved their trust.

Once when we visited the three of them, we were blessed to be graced by their physical presence. They were close enough to our truck that if I extended my hand outward through the window, I was able to reach them easily. Nebu was right in front of me, and by softly gazing at her, I experienced an unbreakable bond between the Royal Trinity that was filled with love and the rapture of unconditional joy.

And I was unable to help but wonder, *Does love such as this truly exist in the world?*

Will I, one of these days of my life, experience love and rapture of unconditional joy as deep as this divine being right in front of me?

Before I could complete the question that was in my heart, I heard a faint voice, which I was pretty certain was Nebu's, whispering in the background of my mind: "Love thyself!"

Those of us who have embarked on a spiritual journey must have heard at some point that to love others, we must first love ourselves.

Love myself? What does that even mean?

I was mostly lost and confused during the early days of my spiritual journey. Loving who I was unconditionally sounded so easy, but it was the hardest thing to do. I didn't know where to start. I had very little reference to understand what that truly meant, and very few practical steps to do so. Often, the love for oneself is considered self-centered, but perhaps I had misunderstood that altogether.

I thought that love existed outside of myself and I needed to *do* something or *be* someone to gain it. I constantly felt the need to prove myself. The harder things were, the more deserving of love I felt. I thought it was something that was promised if I behaved well or performed great.

After doing this dance repetitively, I realized that this way of operating delivered more frustration and agony rather than love or connection. I was feeling empty from within, constantly seeking love and happiness through external pursuits.

And I wasn't the only one.

I keenly observed that we were *all* looking in the wrong direction. In the process of pursuing love and happiness externally, we were unintentionally creating more destruction in the world—with others and with ourselves.

Over the years, I was busy figuring out this self-love thing. I had many desires when it came to love.

I wanted it all.

I wanted the nurturing love of a mother, the guiding love of a mentor, the companionable love of siblings and friends, the deep romantic love of a sensual feminine partner, the warmth of belonging within my family and community, the passionate love of adventures and creativity, the spiritual love of interconnectedness, and all the other subtle and ineffable forms of love that were yet to be discovered. I deeply desired the full spectrum of love, but I wasn't able to articulate what I wanted. I had always known that those desires were reasons to be fully alive—to first and foremost experience the depths of love and then share it with the world. I believed that love was, after all, part of the wonder and ordinary magic of life.

However, I had an inner conflict.

I knew what I wanted, but because I didn't know how to describe it, I wasn't able to ask for it. I was *afraid* to ask for it. I wanted love in all expressions to be given to me unconditionally. I thought it was promised. And when these expectations weren't met, life felt unfair. Drowning in self-pity, I didn't want to make any changes in order to pursue it.

Why should I?

I wanted to exist in a world where all of us were already expressing those forms of love. The world I knew didn't sound very much like that, though. As a highly sensitive child, I was constantly bewildered when I discovered that the world didn't match up to my expectations.

Growing up, I learned that it was naïve to give, receive, and express love unconditionally. Instead, it was transactional and something to be earned. The common assumption was that everyone was out there to take advantage of me and no one deserved the benefit of the doubt.

Hence, love was blind and foolish, and it had to be managed carefully.

The belief that the world was predatory led so many people I knew to play appalling games with one another. I constantly heard stories about those who cheated and preyed on each other. There were also accounts of those who'd given up on love altogether, or had doubled down on their efforts and worked so hard just to show others that they deserved love. Also, there were those apathetic ones on the sidelines, judging those who were desperate for love as foolish beings. There were myriad participants in the game of love, and so many were wounded.

Playing with love was like playing with fire—once bitten, twice shy. The paradigm of love from the eyes of the victim perpetuated, and it was self-sustaining. When we felt hurt, we ended up hurting others despite our greatest intentions.

It felt like there was no way out!

Guidance from adults wasn't helpful. The adults were as lost as the children because they had not even figured out what love meant for themselves yet. Consequently, the many expressions of love became extremely convoluted, and there was little to no openness to explore anything beyond the context that was set in stone by social expectations.

Being a highly sensitive child, I enjoyed expressing my emotions. But at some point, I learned that it was shameful for men to be so open about their emotions. Emotions and sensitivity were seen as signs of weakness.

I was taught not to cry because big boys didn't cry.

I was taught not to be angry and impulsive because kind boys controlled their temper.

I was taught not to be gentle and sweet in expressing love because being gentle and sweet made me less "manly."

I was taught to stop needing hugs and kisses because strong boys weren't needy.

So, out of fear of being called a sensitive, feminine boy, I hid all of my emotions under the rug and put up a stoic face all of the time. I thought this was the way to win in the game of love. If I was able to show off my brawn, my brains, and my cool personality to the world, then I was able to be loved, praised, acknowledged, and someday have my innermost desires fulfilled.

There were so many expectations people needed to fulfill when it came to being loved by others. One of them was to live up to a certain standard of beauty. We all thought we had to look a certain way, with a certain body shape, and with a certain attitude, in order to be loved.

People were mostly afraid to say out loud how inconveniently disproportionate all of us looked. We stayed silent out of politeness. However, such politeness was mostly inauthentic, because truthfully, our appearances weren't made equal, and they could never measure up to the "standards of beauty" that were created by the advertising and marketing industries. Unintentionally, we started to look at our bodies with a distorted perception. Looking beautiful became a silent pressure that we internalized and tortured ourselves with.

If only someone had told me earlier that looking good had nothing to do with winning approval or love from others. Sadly, I picked up the opposite message at a very young age, and my appearance turned into an obsession when I turned into a full-fledged adolescent.

I was overly self-conscious and afraid that the way I looked wasn't good enough for others. If that wasn't bad enough, I was worried that the flaky red skin on my face and body would turn people off. I spent every moment deprecating myself when I looked in the mirror, always wishing for a better body image and facial appearance. I thought that my looks were mediocre, so I had to work hard on my other qualities to become more lovable. I diligently tried to be good at sports, academics, music—and I wanted my personality to be engaging. Little did I know that the person I was trying to be was no more than a facade, a reflection of others' expectations, which made me feel like a chameleon who never fit in anywhere.

I became a people pleaser. Somehow I knew what others wanted to hear from me, and I knew what I "should" say. Mothers of my friends enjoyed my company because I was such a sweet and mature young boy who paid respect to his elders. My female friends confided their deepest secrets in me because I was attentive and trustworthy. Despite that, I was constantly "friend zoned" and had little luck in experiencing puppy love during my teenage years. Internally, I felt claustrophobic but shoved those feelings away. And from time to time, with self-introspection, ghastly thoughts reminded me of how much of an impostor I was.

The capitalist society showed me another perspective on love: people were able to buy and win love by offering gifts to each other. However, I felt that giving and receiving gifts was short-lived and superficial. Perhaps I missed the point, as I cared more about the value of companionship and unintentionally misunderstood the art of gifting. This misunderstanding made the generous gesture of giving gifts seem perverse. For me, giving gifts became a strategic way to get someone's attention and avoid extremely vulnerable situations.

I was a shy teenage boy who wasn't able to utter a single word in front of my crushes, so I wrote letters and cards to express myself, and also bought fancy gifts to win over girls' hearts. I used to place gifts where my crush was sitting in the classroom and then, *poof!*—I disappeared, nowhere to be found. Meanwhile, I waited anxiously for a reply.

Deep down, I was afraid of rejection and getting hurt. My cowardly acts were met with either a shy recipient who wasn't able to say thank you, or someone who was afraid to accept my offer. Growing up, I didn't know why it was such a big deal for a girl to accept or reject a gift with romantic intentions in a straightforward manner. It was only later in my adolescent years that I realized that the object of my romantic interest had to go through an impossible dilemma. On the one hand, if she accepted the gift, then by default, she had to accept me as a romantic partner, even if she didn't want to. On the other hand, if she rejected the gift, then she had to reject me entirely and end up hurting me while losing the friendship that we had, even if she didn't want to do that, either.

I had heard stories of girls who lied to themselves and decided to give in to inauthentic relationships by people-pleasing.

I also heard stories of girls completely ignoring the boys who were interested in them, leaving them confused and hanging, with so many questions. I found that most of the girls I knew weren't able to communicate clearly and were afraid to say the taboo word *no*—most of the time, for good, protective reasons. It was rare to hear stories of girls who outright rejected another boy confidently.

I could only imagine what it was like to be a woman in a dysfunctional man's world. However, despite my vivid imagination, I was never truly able to understand what it felt like to be in their shoes.

As for me, I was completely ghosted as a form of rejection, while at the same time, they would take the gift.

Sad, yes, but I deserved it, anyway.

I learned from experience to simply not buy gifts unless I was earnest and intentional. Because once the act of gifting was complete, it was a spin of the roulette wheel: either the end of a friendship or the beginning of an intimate relationship. There was nothing in between. Most of the time, it signified the end of a friendship, which left my poor, sensitive heart in despair and eventually immersed in self-hatred.

We were all by-products of a systemic dysfunction when it came to expressing and receiving love from each other. Our society at that time had a dim awareness of the importance of emotional intelligence, and consequently, many of us youth had very little skillful means to navigate our emotional vulnerability. We were so afraid to get hurt; thus, we weren't able to be firm with our communications of love. As a result, we hid our true faces from each other.

As an adolescent growing into a young adult, I developed an inferiority complex that made me a perfectionist. Along with that, I experienced the fear of complacency, which felt like I didn't work hard enough. And if I didn't work hard enough, I wasn't able to prove that I was worthy of love.

I was afraid to be unwanted and abandoned, so rejection was something I habitually ran away from. Driven by fear, I didn't see rejection as a firm boundary or a message to back off from others, but a wall to be broken through and to conquer. Such denial made me a persistent lover, and maybe a narcissistic one. This made me the perfect representation of the phrase "Needy people are scary people."

I figured out that one of the reasons this had happened to me was because my basic human need for love and authenticity had been unmet. No one had taught me that rejection was okay and how to move through such a difficult human experience adequately. When memories of rejection were unprocessed and such needs were left unattended, these emotions finally sank into my unconscious and took possession of my conscious will.

I ended up becoming an actual *monster of love*.

Fear of rejection became the very reason why I hardened my personality further. I was very unkind to myself and took on more burdens than I was actually capable of carrying. I felt the need to become the heroic figure and be a powerful savior to others. Responsibility for others became my love language. I enjoyed the feeling of being needed. This false enjoyment gave me a false sense of empowerment.

Wounded people were as attracted to me as I was to them. I made them feel better temporarily, only to realize that I was feeding a black hole. It never took long for the roles to reverse when the savior fell from grace, whose energy got depleted and eventually became the victim.

The disillusionment shattered when my ex-partners weren't able to return the love I was giving. I swore many times not to return to such an unhealthy relationship dynamic, but I kept returning no matter how conscious I was of the red flags. The problem was, I kept looking for red flags in others when I should have looked for them within myself.

There were many points in my life when I wanted to give up on relationships altogether, deciding that I was better on my own. Being a lone wolf sounded promising. As a confused young adult, I had already come to the conclusion that love was bleak, false, and a pretense that many of us made up to make ourselves feel better about life.

Yet, as I watched Nebu gaze at me, the wonder and ordinary magic emanating from her being penetrated deep into my soul. The love from her simply didn't allow me to settle with that conclusion.

I thought I had come here to learn about leadership.

How does love or loving myself have anything to do with leadership?

Perhaps there was no way out until I dealt with the truth of the matter. The only way out was *through*. I had to confront the dysfunctional love operating system that had been running amok all my life.

CHAPTER ELEVEN
Awkward Lessons of Loving Vulnerably

In 2013, I had a dream in which I had a difficult time differentiating what was real and what was imaginary. In it, I met a beautiful girl who had all the qualities I desired, and the intimacy we shared was euphoric. It was pure bliss. It was surreal, but the images were also incredibly vivid. My heart felt completely open, and my senses were tingling all over my body, such that I had difficulty waking up and getting out of the bed. It was as if the complex emotions from the dream held me prisoner, thanks to a potent potion of lust and longing.

It was also a time when spiritual and mystical experiences were completely new to me, so I had no understanding about the changes I was going through. I wasn't taking any type of psychedelics, yet I was constantly experiencing altered states of consciousness. I had no idea how they were activated, but my subtle energy systems seemed to be rising and waking up.

It was both cathartic and ecstatic, painful and euphoric. The only desire I had was to remember this dream, especially who and what about it had fulfilled my innermost desires. I wanted to manifest this dream into reality, to return to the wonder and ordinary magic of aliveness.

Awakened by such ecstasy, I dived right in to try to understand this experience. I googled the meaning of dreams and found that there were many references about them having premonitory qualities. The issue with my human mind was that once it had an explanation that was colored with strongly attached emotions, I stopped seeing other ways of interpretation. I kept affirming that the meaning of my dream was that I was going to meet someone new who was going to make me feel complete.

The mind works in such a way that once a powerful conscious intention is set, it starts to create connections, and the Universe conspires with it to manifest that intention. The reticular activating system, an intriguing part of the brain, starts to filter information that matches the intention. As a result, I experienced a magnetic quality to my thoughts for the very first time: I started attracting people, situations, and circumstances that matched the vibration of my thoughts. I learned that intention was both direction and vibrational, which allowed what I sought within my deepest desire to be seeking *me*.

The premonition manifested into reality when the girl of my dreams showed up a week later. She was a stranger to my eyes but familiar to my heart. I seemed to know her without knowing a single thing about her. Her entire embodiment reflected the same features as the girl in my dreams, and her character was uncannily similar.

Instantly, the concoction of lust and longing that had held me prisoner was emptied, and the love potion was injected into the arteries and veins of my cardiovascular system. I lost my sense of logic when these hormones took over.

I thought love at first sight was nonsense until that moment. I then concluded that dating this person was a miracle and part of a divine plan. It felt destined. Being a New Age newbie, I obsessively searched everything I was able to find on the internet about soul mates, birth-date compatibility, tarot, numerology, and anything I was able to get my hands on to affirm my feelings.

Again, everything seemed to fit perfectly.

We were meant to be!

Yet, I ran in the opposite direction. I was too shy to speak, and my wild monkey mind started brainstorming a thousand possible ways to introduce myself. The thing about unexpressed, strong emotions is that when left unattended, they often turn into obsession. The further I repressed these strong feelings, the more my obsession turned into possession. I was definitely possessed by my own delusions.

After many weeks, I finally got up the courage to speak to my dream girl. We had met through a dance club at university, and I was self-conscious about how bad I was at dance. I wanted to impress her, but nothing that I did or said felt good enough. I supposed this was typical for people with inferiority complexes.

At last, I came up with an excellent idea: choreographing a dance routine together and putting on a show as a group. I would have a perfect reason to spend time with her.

My love story didn't go far, though.

It was unrequited love. And I felt completely unnoticed.

Well, of course!

I never came clean or vulnerably expressed the feelings I had for her. I was trying to protect myself, but at the same time, I tried to show my affection for her with 10,000 petty hints. I spent time making myself look good, giving her gifts, caring for her, and talking about things we were passionate about.

Nevertheless, all of this felt futile.

No matter how much effort I put in, I was never able to look her in the eye to simply confess how I felt, vulnerably and authentically. I knew that if I *had* confessed, she would have told me no, yet I was in denial.

I was afraid to face the music because if I did, then that would mean that my dream had been untrue. And if that was the case, then there was no such thing as true love in this world. But if I never gave it a chance, then I couldn't fail. I wanted my dreams of wonder and ordinary magic to last a little longer, and maybe forever. Hence, it was better to bury my feelings further because I wasn't able to bear the possibility of being rejected.

In a self-destructive manner, I allowed my entire system to become paralyzed, and my heart swung between fierce palpitations and numbness. There were days when I tried to muster up the courage to tell her how I felt, but I was thwarted by panic attacks. I wanted to get it over with and move on, but I never did.

Thus, I got stuck.

I wasn't at all kind or loving to myself in this situation. I was both embarrassed and filled with self-hatred. I buried myself in self-defeating thoughts; pushed myself to the brink of exhaustion in my physical training; and tortured myself with constant, conflicting emotional turmoil.

In due time, I got depressed, filled myself with self-loathing, and was consequently invaded by suicidal thoughts. Despite needing help, I continued to hide from the world. I blamed myself for having chronic atopic dermatitis, and I hated life for making me draw the short stick. I was drowning in my emotional mess without anyone noticing, because I told not a single soul about my problems. I looked fine on the outside but was crumbling on the inside. I was very good at hiding.

Drunk on a delusional love potion, I found expectations of love completely distinct from reality. I was disoriented, and life didn't make sense anymore. I wallowed in my disappointment and became addicted to my self-defeating behaviors. The emotional turmoil grew, and I felt a growing rage within me toward God and life itself. I already had enough pain with my health circumstances and didn't need any more of it.

Life is unfair.

Why was I made to fall in love when this was an unrequited love?

My heart was torn apart and inside out.

The craziest truth to accept was this: *no one did this to me but me.* It took me forever to own that. I had to take responsibility for my life if I didn't want to continue to be in self-destruct mode.

Having my heart broken was part of the journey to become an emotionally mature human being. I came to learn that *a broken heart is an open heart.* For love to *emerge* from within, what I previously understood to be love had to *die.* The delusions, the mystical concepts, the beautiful philosophies, the fantasies, and all the ideas I had about love...had to die and be transformed.

In fact, I knew nothing about love until I met death at the front door in 2016.

Three years had passed since I had been drunk in that delusional love potion, and I'd kept myself sane by not falling in love again. I had done so by pouring all of my passionate energy into dance instead, and it had gotten me somewhere.

I had reached a certain level of mastery where I didn't need to overthink how my body moved, and I began to feel comfortable in my own skin. It was the first time in my life that I actually felt proud of myself for achieving something. As an overachiever, I never celebrated or even acknowledged my victories. Thus, being proud of something about myself for the very first time was actually exciting. This made me consider the possibility that dance and movement could actually be my career. Academics became my secondary priority, while learning dance and engaging in the movement arts became my primary focus.

Regretfully, this happiness and these exhilarating emotions didn't last very long before a series of deathlike events came knocking on my door.

The first event was the "death" of a dance team I had fallen in love with because it had given me a dream that I never thought I could have. Now, after one season together, the team was breaking apart and was moving in different directions.

The dance team had broken off during the summer, so I

decided to continue to pursue my dance journey alone. I was extremely frustrated, because I had experienced countless examples of abandonment in the past from friends who were on this very same path. Many saw the performing art of dance as a side project that they engaged in and never continued when things got too hard or required too much commitment of time, energy, attention, and money. In fact, most felt the need for a safety net. Basically, dance wasn't able to feed their tummies or pay the bills.

I, on the other hand, saw dance as my world. It was my everything, but I was afraid to claim it as such because of parental expectations about completing my university degree and getting a normal job. I was finally achieving some level of mastery in my movements, but it felt like I was always one step slower than I should be. Hence, I never really had a chance to prove how good I was at it.

If only I had been this impressive when I met that girl of my dreams, then maybe I would have been confident enough to express my love.

If only I had been a better a teammate, then maybe the dance team would have continued.

If only I could give myself a chance to focus on dance completely, then maybe I could do this for a living. How far could I go if I actually gave myself a serious chance to go all out in my passion for dance?

Creating assumptions and "if only" scenarios only made things worse. I was constantly torn between expectations and reality. There was never a time when I felt that my imperfections were acceptable.

I was always late for something.

The second event came abruptly when I received a call that

very same summer. It was from an old friend who was acquainted with the girl of my dreams. We all used to dance together.

I heard my friend's solemn voice and knew that some kind of bad news was about to reveal itself.

"She passed away in a bus accident," my friend said.

In that moment, time and space slowed down, and I dropped into the eternal now.

I knew who she was talking about, but I still asked, "Who?" My cool tone was a form of denial.

The old friend mentioned the name of the girl of my dreams, explained how it had all unfolded, and invited me to attend her funeral if I was interested. I was on the opposite end of the globe, and I knew it was impossible for me to make drastic changes to take the next flight.

Hearing this news caused all the hurt that was buried beneath my heart to resurface. I was confused again because pain came from all sorts of directions with different contexts. One form of it came from the unresolved, unrequited love for my dream girl. Another came from her death and the fact that I had just lost someone important in my life. There was also the pain of losing all opportunity to reconnect with her when I'd finally become a more confident person. Last, there was the pain of regret, because I had lived so cowardly all my life and had not been able to express my love to the people around me, especially to her. I wished I had spoken my truth and had mustered up the courage to profess my love confidently before the end came.

Her death reminded me that I wasn't *living*—I was a person going through my life half-heartedly in everything that I did, promised, and thought about. The funny thing about grief for me was that I didn't become all sentimental and depressed right away.

Instead, I was filled with rage and anger.

This time, it was on me.

One month later, the third event came when I heard news of my eldest uncle's death from a heart attack. The timing had just gotten more eerie. It was as if the Grim Reaper was nearby.

I had never felt so vulnerable as when I saw my father crumbled from within. I didn't have plans to return home to Malaysia, but this incident gave me an opportunity to reconnect with my family.

After all, life was fleeting.

I was trying to make sense of all the death that was occurring all around me, and I wondered why it had to happen now. A loss of a family member made me more appreciative of my familial connections, and I wondered what it meant to cultivate authentic connections with others.

I had always been at odds with my family. I never knew what that was about, but I never seemed to be able to open up to anyone completely, except my mother. As a child, I got the impression from my family that I was a sickly, broken child with special privileges. As such, it seemed that my family members treated me with a mixture of pity and jealousy.

That made me put up a shell of protection, because people weren't seeing me for me, but rather, were seeing what they thought I was by seeing the surface. Maybe my illness reminded them of the suffering that they were trying to hide in their own lives. This made me feel like an inconvenient presence when I was around others.

Now, as I confronted my past with a new perspective, I realized that there were way too many assumptions that I had made up out of my victimhood. I didn't know if the phenomenon of death was a curse or a blessing, but these assumptions about my family were dispelled when a death of this family member came too soon. For the very first time, I was able to feel the love and care we actually had for each other. We just didn't have the skillful means to communicate those feelings to each other.

Death opened up my perspective about how many of us habitually learn to numb our painful feelings. I watched people at my uncle's funeral trying so hard to be strong by repressing their tears. I thought that was a weird definition of strength.

I saw this type of inhibition of emotions with respect to the experience of loss and the fight against vulnerability as some form of pathology that was brewing in the background of modern society. It was a dysfunction of our societal behaviors that eventually led us to disease and disharmony. That reflection showed me why I was not able to express my emotions to the girl of my dreams, as well as why I wasn't able to cope with any form of loss or rejection.

The experience of attending a funeral for the very first time in my life was unnervingly solemn. After I left the service, I saw dullness in people's eyes everywhere I went. They weren't quite living. They were distracted by the virtual world, hungry for more dopamine hits. They were ignorant of their emotions, also wishing that they didn't have to feel anything but superficial pleasure, which was often mistaken for happiness.

And I asked myself, *Who are the ones who are truly living?*

The dead who are fully liberated from this world, or the living who are trapped in this world?

After those incidents in 2016, every time I met someone whom I was able to connect with on any level of attraction, I simply expressed my true feelings. I no longer had anything to lose. I completely swung to the opposite extreme.

From not expressing any ounce of my feelings, I went in the other direction and expressed all of myself. I sometimes came across to people as overly intense. At that stage of my evolution to understand love and relationships, I thought it was better to jump into a relationship quickly so that I could discover if the partnership was a good fit right away.

Mostly, it was a reactive behavior that was protecting me. I didn't have to repeat my past by expressing my emotional attachment to a person for too long. Reflecting upon my behavior now, I realize that my expressions came off with such intensity because there was a hunger within me to experience deep love.

For this reason, I continued to be blind.

I didn't pause to consider or sit within my feelings to differentiate the type of connection I was having. The hunger for an authentic soul connection blindsided me and made me ignore many relationship red flags. I took any opportunity to connect when someone had an interest in me.

I suddenly went from being a person who got his heart broken all the time to a heartbreaker. Intimacy developed quickly because of strong attraction on the soul level, but it was always too fast, too soon. The moment I received closeness and intimacy from my partner, I felt the need to run away and scream out loud for my personal space.

As I was becoming more authentic with my own needs, I also got to know how eccentric and weird my daily life looked compared to other people. My health condition required me to live in a very healthy way. I was willing to spend a lot of money on organic food, worked on any form of biohacking that I was able to get my hands on daily, and took energy-healing and life-coaching sessions frequently. These habits made me a personal-growth freak, and I was someone who required high maintenance as well. I was highly sensitive; I needed a cold, dark room to sleep in; and I had a hard time adapting to any new routine. Having a partner in my life meant that all these habits had to be disrupted, yet disrupting them wasn't good for my physical and emotional well-being.

I had always thought that it was extremely unfair for someone to subscribe to my health ideals. However, at the same time, if my partner wasn't able to appreciate the same ideals that I did, our relationship never would have worked out. I found myself in constant conflict, balancing between my own needs and those of others. And that balancing act was a lifelong practice of relationship yoga that I needed to learn.

Because of all these peculiar and particular needs, I used to think that the only way a relationship could work for me was if it was with someone who subscribed to similar spiritual teachings and forms of healthy living. As intensely as I dived into relationships, I also became extremely picky in choosing my intimate partners. I was seeking a perfect person who'd be able to resonate with everything that I was. I went so far as to describe this person on paper to initiate the manifestation process. Yet making such a list was exactly the limitation that was stopping me from experiencing true love.

Why?

Again, I was falling into that trap of trying to find love *outside* of me, when what I needed was to fulfill something *within* me. After death showed up, I learned to embrace life more. I made more mistakes, but the regret of making them was never worse than the regret of holding back love and playing the game of life too safely. I learned the lessons to love awkwardly along the way, just like a baby who was learning how to walk. The only difference was that I didn't have a mentor or a guide to emulate, unlike the infants who had their parents.

At least I was making a change now, attempting to figure out this love equation.

I promised myself that I had to learn to have courage in order to be vulnerably openhearted, and have clarity of vision to discern which relationships to invest in and which relationships to let go of. Being vulnerably openhearted was to be fully alive, and it was okay that I didn't know how to do so yet.

But that didn't mean that I had to be in a hurry and grasp on to love every time I got the chance. I had to learn discernment, the practice of listening deeply to the heart, because it always knows the next best step before the interference and interruption of the wild monkey mind.

The death of important people around me caused a part of me to die a little too, but new parts of me were being born in the process. I felt that this aspiration was the only way I'd be able to pay a tribute to those who had passed. I was grateful that death looked out for me while I was still alive and not during the end of my time on Earth. The fearful little child who was too shy to express love took his first step that year.

And we all know what taking first steps in anything feels like. They are clumsy and awkward. Yet through death, my love story turned from seeking love outside of myself to seeking it within me.

Love was never a noun, but a verb. It was all about choosing to meet the suffering of the human experience with total loving awareness. By walking this path, and before meeting my own death, I hoped to find out that I was the love that I was seeking all along.

CHAPTER TWELVE

Leading Through Fire
with an Open Heart

Memories of the past streamed through me as if they were yesterday. In the final month of 2018, in the middle of the bushveld of Timbavati, I wondered if I had actually learned anything over the many of years of my spiritual studies. I seemed to have forgotten the lessons of the past and the promises I had made to myself.

As I continued to reflect on the profound changes I *had* actually made, I hardened further with self-hatred. I felt that I had received a reality check, and that the profound pain of the past would keep repeating itself if I didn't radically change. I was frustrated with my human condition of forgetfulness, as well as my avoidance in dealing with the truth of the matter— I was still afraid to love and let love in.

Instead, over the past two years, I had continued to chase

after the next spiritual high that took me further away from true love. And that made me feel sick in my gut.

In that moment of honest reflection, I felt a deep yearning to integrate the difficult lessons of the past. I didn't want to just be aware of these spiritual lessons—I wanted to be able to embody their qualities by changing and transforming them.

I wanted to purify my soul through the spiritual fire of true love so that all the distortions and dysfunctional operating systems of love could be transformed into the true spiritual gold that I was seeking. I knew so much, but I'd made little to no progress in creating actual change.

I also knew that once this trip with the lions was over and I returned to my old environment, if my conditioned mind hijacked my growth process, I would be forced to return to square one. These limitations had always been gnawing at the back of my mind, and I felt helpless in the face of them.

Nonetheless, although it was uncomfortable, an honest truth dawned on me. In a moment of sobriety, I saw clearly what was possible. A fire was ignited within my heart, and I was determined to make a change. And the change I was about to make had to be radical.

As I continued to be starstruck by Nebu's beauty and elegance, I asked her a question in my heart, hoping for a clear-cut answer: *What do I do, Nebu?*

My self-victimizing trance was interrupted by a baseline shift at the bushveld, which prompted Assegaia to move from his spot. Watching the young king elegantly move reminded me of how much power there was in a quiet presence. Everyone's eyes were on him, and we were all mesmerized by his graceful demeanor. He had a sense of being comfortable in his own skin, emanating an energy that communicated that he truly belonged in his world. He was within his own lion's heart—it was self-evident, and no judgments would be able to take that away from him.

If not for his mane, I would have mistaken Assegaia for a female because of the soft, nurturing quality that he carried within him. However, there was the presence of great strength, as if he had been born to protect and to provide safety. He had a strong back, a soft front, and a wild heart—so wild that he reminded all of us that he was still a beast of nature. He was completely open, always listening, and attuned to the present moment, which made his commanding presence extend over a large area of the bushveld, as if he were saying, "I am here!" Most important, he looked like he was completely in love with himself.

Ah!

Love myself!

The radical change that I'm looking for is to turn the love within and come home to myself!

I suddenly remembered the message I had received from Nebu. In an instant, all the fragmented memories and reflections came together into one single insight, like separated puzzle pieces that joined together to form a greater picture. I was now able to see the entire image of my life.

Little did I know that there was a golden thread that was guiding me from one experience to another, leading me from one realization to the next in a woven tapestry of my life's destiny. I realized that my fate was to understand the meaning of true love so deeply that I would be able to embody the expression of *Homo luminous* effortlessly. Henceforth, I was to go about living in the world, illuminating the same possibilities that exist in the nature of another. It didn't matter what I chose to do, but *how* I performed those activities—that is, the intention behind them. I was to embody my very own wonder and sense of ordinary magic, and dedicate my life force to sharing that energy with others. Spontaneously, I saw that behind all of my previous suffering was, again, the Divine Grace of the Universe.

It suddenly made sense to me how Nebu and Zihra were both able to recover from their grief after losing Mandla, and how they grew to accept Assegaia as part of their pride. Assegaia's presence was incredibly healing and trustworthy. Instead of using force or dominance to resolve conflict, he exhibited a form of power that was all about collaboration and compassion.

Rather than the *power-over* paradigm that I frequently saw in masculine environments—be it in the business world or in competitive sports—Assegaia was affirming something completely different. He resolved his struggle with the *power-with* paradigm, which was centered in collaboration and creating win-win outcomes.

Assegaia's stance for a new paradigm of leadership that was backed by such love was the very direction I was determined to discover and emulate. However, this was only possible when there was a foundation of the power within—the love for oneself unconditionally. Strangely, it was the furthest thing from being self-centered.

This kind of self-love was almost nonexistent among men in our modern society. We were all striving to prove that we deserved love via external metrics: money, fame, trophies, possessions, and whatever we were able to conquer. This actually made us weak and fragile from within. Instead of protecting our loved ones and our dear Earth, we ended up hurting them with brutal, aggressive acts.

I saw now that true power never comes from the outside but from within. It has nothing to do with fighting or making things right, but rather, softening the heart through humility. And only within that softening can the heart open vulnerably to receive spontaneous insights and stimulate creativity to resolve the matter at hand. An open heart also allows for the wonder and ordinary magic that is already within us and all around us to conjure up miracles of healing and transformation.

Perhaps this was why that Shangaan shaman (whose name was Maria Khosa and carried the mantle of "The Lion Queen of Timbavati") was able to save Linda Tucker and her friends from the pride of lions while carrying a baby on her back.

Perhaps that is what Linda embodies. It is what empowered her to beat the odds and return the white lions to their original kingdom. It gave her the courage to stand up against the nefarious cuddle-to-kill industry and initiate worldwide healing by shining a light on the commoditizing of nature.

Perhaps that is what it means to be *lionhearted*. As defined by Linda, lionheartedness is that quality of fearlessness inspired by love and respect for our natural world that enables us to change our human world for the better. Love, then, isn't just a leadership quality but an act of leadership in itself: *To love is to lead, and to lead is to love.*

This is the Divine Grace of the Universe at work!

The golden thread I received was the law of love and respect for nature, and it began with the unconditional self-love I had known so well as a child: as wonder and ordinary magic. With self-love, protection by the law of love and respect for nature was automatically established for all of us. No degree of darkness in the world could ever take away that light within us. Instead, unconditional self-love birthed the radical acceptance of darkness because it was the very same darkness that showed us the way back to love, light, and truth.

With this realization, I felt as if I were on a precipice, awaiting another profound transformation that would offer me an illuminating answer.

Maybe my heart already knew before my mind did.

⊞

"Celebrate!"

That was the last parting word that echoed in my consciousness after I completed my time with the Lionhearted Leadership Academy. It was one of the most impactful and memorable stories that I heard from Linda while she was imparting her teachings to us.

Linda was sharing how she struggled to fight against darkness. And "Celebrate!" was the very advice that Maria Khosa had given Linda before her passing.

It sounded counterintuitive in the beginning, but there was actually a deeper wisdom behind it. It wasn't about fighting fire with fire, or fighting evil with another necessary evil. These methods had never once shifted the paradigm, as shown in our human history. In fact, such methods only perpetuated and accelerated the wheel of self-destruction.

Celebration was about bringing out the wonder and ordinary magic that lay dormant within us and all around us. Celebration with love was what activated wonder and ordinary magic, and the more of us who participated, the greater its power to create healing in our bodies, and effect transformational change in the world.

Evil was infectious. But love was even more so.

Inspired by the depths of this indigenous wisdom, Linda dared her soft and open heart to move forward, led her team through the fire, and ignited the flame of love within the collective consciousness. This was what it meant to be in "alion-ment" to nature. And through this alignment, what was impossible from the mind became possible from the heart. With that, *intuition now guided the intellect.*

I left the heartlands with bittersweet feelings. As excited as I was to restart my life with a new perspective, I felt sad because I didn't know when I'd receive another opportunity to return to the lions.

This marked the completion of my spiritual journeys abroad, and it was my turn to pick up the torch, step into a leadership role, and become a powerful change agent in the world, beginning with the local community where I lived. I was feeling hopeful and optimistic about this upcoming chapter of my life. Even though I didn't know what to expect next, at least I knew that I was able to trust and keep myself centered and aligned with the great teachings of nature's law of love and respect.

I met an extraordinary lady in the midst of the COVID-19 pandemic when social interactions were limited to virtual spaces. It was already a year and a half after the first lockdown in 2020, when wearing masks was the norm, and social distancing was in place.

The dating culture had moved onto apps, and that was how our fates intertwined. Without dancing back and forth

■■
■■

for too long on a particular dating app, we decided to meet at a park, where it was safe to maintain social distancing.

I asked her out right away because I didn't enjoy guessing games in dating apps. It was almost impossible to tell what people were feeling over virtual screens. I thought if a person was a right fit to be with me, then she had to at least have the courage to show up authentically. I appreciated transparency.

Close to three years after I had left the heartlands of the white lions, I had gradually become a person who didn't give too much thought about how someone perceived me. I knew that rejection was merely feedback, not a personal attack on my self-worth.

Now that I had come clean about who I was, I felt an inner peace and calmness when it came to meeting new people, especially meeting women whom I was romantically interested in. I was no longer the boy who ran away. The journey of love and death, along with the wisdom of the white lions, had finally turned me from a boy into a man. And I knew that if I operated in such a way, I would be an attractive human being.

The woman I met in the park was nowhere near spiritually conscious or living healthily. She had always desired it, but she didn't really think it was possible until she met me. She was the kind of person who never got over Disney princesses and retained the wonder and ordinary magic she had experienced as a kid. Authentic to her heart, she was stubborn about keeping performing arts in her life. She wanted to be onstage, to be in the limelight, so that she could remind others of their own wonder and ordinary magic.

She was one of those rare humans who thought her wonder and ordinary magic was more important to keep than abiding to society's expectations of growing up, but she still struggled as a result of the pressure she felt. She wanted to keep her vulnerable heart open, and such openness without a sturdy core of values and inner power made her a target to be bullied and taken advantage of.

She lacked experience in the matter of spirituality and what it meant for her to self-actualize. Despite that, there was resilience and intelligence within her that knew what it meant to have the courage to be vulnerably openhearted in a world that feared truth and authenticity.

She was an empty cup, where most people were full of ideologies and philosophies about love. She knew about the truth of the matter even though she wasn't able to articulate it very well.

I thought that was extremely precious, and that was what drew me to her.

This woman wasn't afraid when she didn't understand the spiritual things that popped out of my mouth from time to time. Instead, she leaned in with eagerness to learn, and asked me to further articulate what I was expressing. She was completely absorbed, and listened to me attentively just to understand who I was and what my world was like.

She didn't compare my journey as a human being to her own. She didn't shy away from me with any inferiority complexes just because I sounded sophisticated. She didn't back away when I called her out for her lack of awareness with respect to certain behaviors, and she wasn't afraid to call me out with my very own words when I did something similar. She made me own my mistakes and my imperfections, and she helped me up when I was down and broken without trying to fix me.

In fact, she helped me work on my mistakes and imperfections without changing me. She simply worked on her own blind spots and self-sabotaging behaviors. And that alone was powerful enough to initiate change within me. She was receptive to my feedback, and she easily caught up to the teachings I shared with her. She reminded me how powerful I was by being the embodiment of the natural wisdom I was gaining from painful human experiences.

In a short time, she owned her power and began to embody her own natural wisdom. That synergy made me change for the better, as I started to know that it was safe for me to be childlike again. The partnership we created was built on lifting each other up to manifest the dreams we were committed to creating in the world. To my surprise, she was doing all of this without a single drop of the spiritual knowledge I had painstakingly searched for throughout my life. Through her, I learned that spirituality and wisdom weren't found in sophisticated books, fanciful conversations, or luxurious retreats—they were found within the simplicity of being fully alive in the moment, trusting wonder and ordinary magic, and opening ourselves up to the Divine Grace of the Universe.

The love we created together required both of us to drop our guards vulnerably, and to soften in the presence of conflict and tension. It was a fierce love that needed both of us to lead each other through the fire. This love was a creative process, with the two of us functioning as equal mirrors that continued to purify our conditioning, forgetfulness, and darkness.

She showed me a dimension of love and connection that I

had never known. I was proven wrong for holding a limiting belief that I needed to be partnered up with someone who was as far along in the human spiritual journey as I was. I thought I needed these qualities to be present in the other so that she could understand, fulfill my needs, and ultimately, love me.

No. There was none of that with her.

In front of each other, we were completely transparent with our thoughts, naked with our emotions, and open in facing life's uncertainties. Romance between us wasn't necessarily comfortable, but rather, it was completely invigorating.

She didn't need me to be the knight in shining armor, even though there were times when that was what she wanted, and how *I* was conditioned to be. And I didn't need her to please me, even though there were times when that was all I wanted and how *she* was conditioned to be.

We practiced saying *no* to each other—not as rejection, but to negotiate so that we came into a deeper yes that met both of our needs. In situations of conflict and disagreement, we agreed to disagree and live our own lives without righteously demanding that one person's ways were better than the other's.

And in times of deep pain and vulnerability, we stayed silent and allowed that space to naturally heal us. It was all about communicating vulnerably with an open heart. When we dropped into that space, all forms of self-righteousness, false assumptions, and victimhood went out the door. That space of nothingness became where the Divine Grace of the Universe could come in and transmute and transform our pain into deeper love. It was also the space where the death of our old definitions of love resurrected into a new form of love, which reflected our new growth as two ordinary humans. The space was a conversation of "us and we" rather than "me versus you."

While I was searching frantically for love, I wasn't able to see it. All the desires that I wanted—the nurturing of a parent, the guidance of a mentor, the companionship of siblings and friends, the deep romantic love of a partner, the warmth and belonging of a community, the passionate love for adventures and creativity, the spiritual love of interconnectedness—were never about what others needed to give me, but qualities of love I wanted to have.

Searching outside of myself reinforced the emptiness within me, as these qualities weren't given a chance to develop until I turned within. Turning within and loving myself had nothing to do with being fulfilled by anything.

It didn't mean that I had to work on the inner aspects of myself in order to be fulfilled.

It didn't mean more mindfulness, more creativity, or more authenticity.

Instead, it was all about the realization and recognition that *Homo luminous* was already within me all along, and unconditional love was undeniably who I was. As a baby, I had always known that, but growing into an adult, I had forgotten that truth. Knowing that I already had the quintessential expression of love within me didn't mean that there was no space for relationships in my life, but just that I didn't need them to fill up my cup anymore. And that was the difference between being an adult and a baby.

Waking up to this truth, I felt completely free. Love became freedom. I found a new opportunity to evolve the existing love operating system and to make new definitions for healthy relationship dynamics.

I had always loved Khalil Gibran's poem "On Marriage," which perfectly reflects how relationship and partnership exist so that both people can walk their journeys individually with honest companionship. Now, *I* had such a relationship, which helped us see each other's true natures and how much love was within us. The relationship was a journey to help each other remember and return back into wholeness, and remember that we were *Homo luminous* all along. We weren't two half beings that needed to fill each other's hearts. Rather, we were two *whole* beings reflecting and mirroring that quintessential expression of love within each other.

Relationships are like yoga. To practice it, we all need to have the courage to be vulnerably openhearted and lead through the fire of conflict, pain, and suffering lovingly. And it begins with us. We have to unlearn and relearn the ways of how we love ourselves.

Love is never something we gain or get from the outside; it is a conscious decision that we make every day to become, express, and offer this gift to others. In return, we need to become true mirrors for each other so that our partner reflects the love that is already within us back to us. And within that reflection is a precious gift, so sweet that all of us dream of it.

That is the love story that we're truly looking for—*to experience the love within ourselves through the act of loving others.*

Love is the celebration of life and of our humanity. Love is how we experience the world through the eyes of the Universe. Love is how we conjure the Divine Grace of the Universe and the wonder and ordinary magic of life. Love is what brings us home to our *extra*-ordinariness.

Through relationships, we are the Universe experiencing its own marvels. And within those marvels are miracles of healing, creation, and transformation beyond our wildest human imagination of what is possible. This is how any of us are able to become leaders who are centered from love with the capacity to create a magnitude of transformation, both in our human and natural worlds.

PART FOUR

Transformation: The Courage to Take Responsibility

"Above all, don't lie to yourself. The man who lies to himself and listens to his own lie comes to a point that he cannot distinguish the truth within him, or around him, and so loses all respect for himself and for others. And having no respect he ceases to love."

—Fyodor Dostoevsky, *The Brothers Karamazov*

CHAPTER THIRTEEN
Emptying My Spiritual Cup

There was an important lesson I had to learn from the Universe before I was rewarded with finding the love of my life and beginning to embody qualities of *Homo luminous*. This was a lesson that could not be found in books, but rather, discovered through living in the trenches of life's pain and suffering. Before the quintessential expression of love could come through my life, some form of ego disintegration had to occur. I realized that all the spiritual glitter of the past that my ego hung on to was apparently not gold. The truth of healing and spirituality was much more ordinary, simple, and definitely *humbling*.

After my time with the white lions in Timbavati, I experienced a strong yearning to return to a place called home, but it was nowhere to be found. I continued to travel to cities wherever my soul called me: Sedona, Austin, San Diego, San

Francisco, Taipei, Milan, Venice, London, and Zurich were all places I visited for a short amount of time—yet none of those cities left me feeling that I was at home. Instead, there was a persistent guilt gnawing at me, like a dark shadow attached to my soul. I knew that it was time for me to finish my education, make my own money, and stop relying on my father's financial aid. Yet my soul-searching wasn't over, and I also knew that I couldn't return home without a promised remedy for the lifelong mysterious illness I had.

Each time I tried to confront the inevitable, it was repelled by a stronger force of avoidance, hoping to delay the reality as long as I was able to. But I knew that if I didn't make some changes soon, the Universe was going to step in and knock me off my current life trajectory anyway. I had learned from experience that changing by choice was always way better than changing reluctantly. The life lessons imposed upon me by the Universe were kind and loving, but they were never nice or comfortable.

The more I traveled, the more I saw that I was clueless about life and where my place on Earth was. I reasoned with myself that maybe I was looking for home in the wrong place to begin with. Perhaps I wasn't actually trying to find a physical home but a spiritual one—a place where I was able to be myself authentically and finally feel a sense of true belonging.

Was this place to be found? Or was it to be created?

I realized that I was homesick for Kuala Lumpur. This was surprising to me, considering how much I enjoyed wandering aimlessly through sauntering. But I had grown exhausted by the costly outward search for home, financially and energetically. Moreover, exhaustion had only made me more depressed, as nowhere seemed right for me. There was a visceral response from my body, which missed being around my Asian heritage. If anything, what I missed was authentic Asian food cooked with local Asian ingredients.

I seriously considered caving in to my strange inner desires to return home to Malaysia, but this also stirred up a lot of us resistance within me. The idea of living there permanently made me queasy on the inside. Thus, an inner conflict started to brew, and not long after that, I had trouble deciphering where my heart wanted me to go. The mind has an uncanny ability to create millions of convincing reasons and voices to confuse the heart.

Life usually happens in two ways: through the motivation of pain or through the motivation of following an inner and intuitive voice of the heart that is connected to a deeper and higher purpose. Obviously, I had not learned anything about pain despite going through so much of it. Consequently, a divine intervention was imposed upon me.

Time was up, and it was right on point.

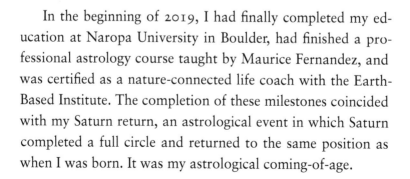

In the beginning of 2019, I had finally completed my education at Naropa University in Boulder, had finished a professional astrology course taught by Maurice Fernandez, and was certified as a nature-connected life coach with the Earth-Based Institute. The completion of these milestones coincided with my Saturn return, an astrological event in which Saturn completed a full circle and returned to the same position as when I was born. It was my astrological coming-of-age.

Symbolically, this represented a time of initiation into adulthood and achieving important milestones in life. It wasn't a unique experience to me alone, but a collective human experience. Prior to a Saturn return, we usually lived our lives based on the expectations of our parents, teachers, mentors, and bosses. And during the Saturn return, major life crises such as health issues, breakups, career changes, relocating to a new geographical region, or spiritual awakenings were liable to occur. For some, the Saturn return influenced just one area of life, but for the lucky ones, the Saturn return was able to influence all of the above. The spiritual lesson here was all about learning how to take full and complete responsibility for our own choices and to live our life in concert with our soul. We weren't made simply to be copies of our predecessors but to integrate the wisdom that we learned from them with our own creative and authentic self-expression. In other words, it was a time for the uncomfortable growing pains of life, and we wouldn't be able to escape them.

At that time, I was thinking about making Boulder my home, so I tried to find my way around. Nevertheless, the more I tried, the more my efforts seemed futile, and nothing was really a perfect fit for me. I wasn't sure which industry I was able to enter with my university degree, coaching certification, and astrology certification besides walking the path of a spiritual guide. Hence, I narrowly set my mind on being a freelance life coach in the field of spiritual health, with astrological expertise.

I knew there would be difficulty applying for a work visa in the United States in this field of work, so I didn't bother trying. Moreover, I didn't have the money for an immigration lawyer to help me out. I felt unsupported and simply gave it up. However, deep down, I knew those were just petty reasons. The truth was that even after five years of living in Boulder, I continued to feel alienated and not like I belonged anywhere. I yearned to return to my roots because I simply didn't know who I was and what my purpose in life was anymore. No matter how far I went to search for those answers, it seemed fruitless. I was tired of being a homeless soul in the world. Despite all the adulting efforts I had made, there were spiritual lessons I had not learned or integrated into my life yet. Graduating from my formal education didn't necessarily mean that I had passed the initiations from my soul and the Universe.

Not long after brooding about my miserable fate, an initiation from the Universe began. Halfway through a wintry February in Boulder, more snow fell, and the temperature plummeted very quickly. Out of nowhere, I experienced excruciating pain that shot up my spine from my lower back. Within a couple of days, I wasn't able to walk and became bedridden.

I had not fallen or experienced a physical impact that would have caused this condition to flare up. I was also experiencing a high fever, my muscles were twitching involuntarily with pain, and I soon felt the life force being sucked out of my body. In addition to the physical agony, I was receiving visions and symbols in my mind that I didn't understand, and I was hearing thoughts that weren't my own.

It felt like psychosis and some sort of spiritual emergency. Some might call it a spiritual attack, but I knew I was moving through a unique type of spiritual initiation that had been created for me by the Universe. I intuitively knew that the more I fought it, the more the situation would worsen. Looking for a doctor and taking medication didn't even come to mind until someone mentioned it, and then I insistently refused to do so. I knew that whatever I was going through wasn't something that allopathic Western medicine would be able to explain or fix.

Following my own research, I made an intuitive guess about what I was experiencing. This condition was called *ukuthwasa* in the African culture, and it was only experienced by select individuals chosen by the Great Spirit, and who were destined to be *sangomas,* or traditional African healers. Some New Age spirituality books also called it the *kundalini* awakening. And I was sure that if I continued to look closely enough across all traditions, they would all have names for this type of initiation, experienced by those destined to be spiritual healers.

It takes one to know one, I guess.

How could anyone learn how to heal others if they don't know what it feels like to experience pain?

I was wondering why these experiences had to happen to me, but at least this time, I wasn't feeling completely lost and helpless. I was already prepared for this moment. I had skills that I had learned from my college programs, as well as my psychedelic experiences with Grandmother Ayahuasca— along with profound wisdom gained from those great sovereign beings, the white lions. As long as I centered myself with the energy of love and went into deep contemplation to understand the message behind my condition, I would be able to free myself from the pain.

But will I die before I figure out this message?

Or will I figure out the message before I die?

Pain was a potent medicine. Although I wasn't able to do much about my situation, I did have the time and space to silently ask the Universe for guidance. That was when the sea of convincing reasons and voices dissipated, and all that was left was the true voice of my heart.

I was only given one word: *home.*

Thinking about home made me think about a certain leopard shaman I had met in 2018, before my trip to the heartlands of the white lions. His name was John Lockley, and he was one of the first white men traditionally initiated by the Xhosa people of South Africa. John was in Boulder to teach a workshop about shamanism, and there would be an opportunity for people to receive a bone divination session (a healing session) with him. Without having a clear intention, I saw this as a golden opportunity to give it a try, just for the sake of experiencing something new. Unintentionally, I was window-shopping spirituality.

Meeting John for the very first time was intimidating. He felt ancient, as if primal forces were running through him. Combining a gentle tone of friendliness with the stern countenance of a wise master, he spoke to me with penetrative words that became a harsh wake-up call. He mentioned that I was very disconnected from my roots and my ancestors and that this was a recipe for breakdowns. My spiritual training couldn't advance if I was lacking the foundation of a connection to my land and roots.

He said, "You are not able to find it here in Boulder. This is the land of the hungry ghost, especially for those who are searching for spirituality."

And I damn well knew he was right. I was offended that he had indirectly called me a hungry ghost, but at the same time, I was humbled by his commitment to truth, and grateful that he didn't sugarcoat what I had to confront in order to free my spirit and return to my spiritual home.

After illuminating me with an inconvenient truth, John poured us some tea. He then spilled the very same tea that he poured onto the floor—intentionally. I continued to be bewildered by him, and my eyes widened.

What is this guy doing now?

"Empty your cup," he told me. "True spirituality comes through when one's cup is empty."

John's bizarre actions and mannerisms made me feel puzzled, causing the denial that had been coursing within me to return. I felt a flush of energy rising within me, and I wanted to speak back to him, but deep down I knew that I had to shut up and listen. We had not even gotten to the bone divination, and it felt like I was already being given an important life lesson.

Right away, Suzuki-roshi's *Zen Mind, Beginner's Mind*, which was part of my reading from contemplative psychology classes, popped up in my mind. I suddenly understood what John was talking about: *beginner's mind*.

The path of spirituality required humility because this human quality helped us to be attentive and create space for deep listening. It was only through such deep listening that the love, grace, and wisdom of the Universe could come through for us. Upon reflection, it was exactly this state of mind that created the right conditions for the self-illuminating conversations I had with the Universe.

Spirituality wasn't all about how much I knew, or what practices I did, or how many special retreats and adventures

I took part in. It was the exact opposite of that. It was the surrendering of the ego—an understanding that it was never able to know any better than how it was programmed, so it better shut up and listen.

The conversation with John made me realize that everything I'd learned over the years in Boulder were mere theories. If I didn't know how to open myself to the orderly chaos of my spirit, I wouldn't be able to understand anything at all. Theories would remain dead and intellectual—rather than living wisdom that was able to invigorate and inspire others. To search for the destined land of belongingness and a spiritual home, I had to begin to unlearn what I knew.

In that moment, I was humbled.

After making sure that my cup was at least emptied a little bit, John then led me into a room to begin the bone-divination ritual. We started off connecting to the present moment and our bodies through deep belly breathing, and I was guided to ask a very specific question quietly within my heart for the ritual.

My question was: *Where is home, and how can I find it?*

Bone divination, as I understood it at that time, involved consulting the spirits for answers and guidance. This was done by throwing animal bones on a spread and interpreting them with the help of a *sangoma*. That was exactly what John did.

Watching him perform something supernatural yet completely ordinary made me realize that no matter how much I searched externally for answers, it was futile. The true answers lay within, waiting for me to discover them. Thus, as expected, not much was revealed because I was already aware of most of my karmic patterns and life lessons. It felt more like a revision, and another kind reminder that I was already on the path that I needed to be on.

I was also able to sense that John kept the bone divination simple and held certain revelations back, as if the Universe had told him to do so.

I had to figure it all out by myself.

At the end of it all, we finished with a cleansing ritual, and I was off to my next adventure, holding John's wise words in my heart.

As I thought about the session with John later on, I realized that the message from my sudden lower-back pain was a calling from the Universe to return home to Malaysia. I had to face my past and reconnect with my roots. I needed to answer the question of who I was and why I was here so that I would finally be able to belong to myself and return to my heart. That was the spiritual home I was looking for!

The moment I made this decision, my pain gradually subsided, and it felt like the Universe made sure I was able to move enough to do whatever I needed to do to return home. Through this incident, I learned the *Don't wait for life to happen to you because it is going to motivate you through pain* lesson the hard way. I guessed that sometimes the stubborn conditioning of being human needed some pain to motivate people to move on with their lives.

I told myself that I never again wanted to be pushed by life in such a manner. I decided that from that moment on, I had to be proactive about making sure things happened from the motivation of my heart's inner voice. I must no longer doubt it. Instead, I had to courageously move into the abyss of the unknown future with absolute faith. The best thing about this whole ordeal was that I didn't need to be completely ready.

Showing up was enough.

It took me two months before I was able to walk again. I saw no doctor and I didn't take any medication except marijuana supplements and topical creams that helped me with their amazing analgesic properties. Even as I struggled between getting out of bed and normal living, I forced myself to pack what I needed in order to travel, and shipped everything else back to Malaysia.

And just like that, I was on my way home.

CHAPTER FOURTEEN

Feeling Uncomfortable in My Own Skin

Returning home to Kuala Lumpur, Malaysia, for the first time after being away for ten years was not a comfortable trip. I was going back to an urban environment where hustle and bustle were business as usual. Terrible traffic, with loud blaring honks and screeching sirens and construction jackhammers were the usual sounds of the city.

What a stark contrast from Boulder!

The lack of nature around this concrete jungle made me feel claustrophobic and suffocated. And the traffic noise irritated my senses. Coming back felt worse than before. With the twenty-four-hour glaring lights of the city contributing to light pollution at night, I lost my bearings from the moon and the stars, which made me lose the connection with my inner intuitive guidance.

I may have been back home, but out of all my travels, I had never felt so out of touch and out of place with the land and the people. The overall energy of the city was dissonant, and the disconnection between body, soul, and spirit showed up in others' unconscious mannerisms and behaviors. As I observed interactions between people, I wasn't sure if they were simply talking over each other or actually having a proper conversation. I noticed that everyone seemed to be living in their own world of their thoughts and regurgitating the very same conversations of the past.

Living in the age of smartphones, people's thought engines were replaced by devices, which did the thinking for them. All of these people were *physically* present, but rarely was anyone actually mentally or emotionally present. Most people walked around with hardened emotional armor on their chests and seemed incapable of relaxing. At first, I was completely taken aback, but it seemed as if I had truly forgotten what it was like to immerse myself in this environment.

The norm seemed to be to opt out from one's true feelings, which might have been a helpful strategy to cope with the angst that people were experiencing in their lives. Watching the way they behaved, it looked like they were always in turbulence. Life was on the go. Everyone was busy getting the next gig, rushing to the next appointment, and looking out for the next opportunity. Talking about work was the usual conversation people had with one another, and it didn't seem as if anyone was able to sit down properly to enjoy a decent meal. The hustle culture seemed to be running the city on autopilot.

Pausing for a moment was barely possible.

What a drag to be here!

Observing the dynamic and pace of the city helped me remember what it was like to grow up in Kuala Lumpur. I remembered that we had all been taught that hard work was the key to our very own promised wonderland. It was the only practical thing to do. Growing up, I was surrounded by people who believed this, and I used to see life in the same way they did. Now I could see that they had confused practicality for rigidity.

In the grind of the city, there was little aspiration for self-actualization and the need to seek deeper meaning. Most people were discouraged from pursuing any of it. Survival needs were prioritized, but most of the time, these needs were mistaken for first-world complaints. Even when these needs were finally met, the switch to seek for deeper meaning was never turned on, as unconscious capitalism continued to rule the life of the city people. There was always the next thing to fix, to help, to make, or to break.

I regularly heard people's complaints and seemingly per-fect reasoning like a broken tape recorder:

"When I'm healthy, then I can travel to where I dream to go."

"When I have enough money, then I can go after my passion."

"When my parents are happy enough, then I can take care of myself."

"When I finally graduate from university, then I can make my own choices."

"When I fulfill what my partner asks me to do, then my relationship will be happy."

And the list went on.

Everything was conditional. I was uncomfortable with the disorienting notion that the purpose of my life extended only as far as what was dictated by such limited social and mental constructs. There was a predictable common narrative about what a good life revolved around: "Be born, go through puberty, do well academically, become an adult, make it into a prestigious university, get a good job, start a family, raise the family, create a successful business, excel in your career, plan for retirement, retire from your job, and enjoy the luxury of life before greeting death at the doorstep." And that was it!

Completely absurd!

After being surrounded by this environment long enough, I began to feel uncomfortable in my own skin. I experienced a reverse cultural shock that had nothing to do with my heritage or ethnicity but the desires and meaningful lifestyle choices that I wanted in comparison to those around me. I had changed drastically over the years, but people who knew me saw me not as I was in front of them now. Rather, they clung to past impressions, and the exchanges that we had the last time we met.

The city boy that I used to be now found the city repulsive, because I had become a so-called *nature boy.*

No one had forced such city lifestyle choices upon me, but with so many people subtly practicing, subconsciously behaving, and emotionally playing out such a narrative, I assumed that I had to follow.

Being highly sensitive, my mind was highly suggestible to any form of mental programming of the collective. This meant that I was able to make and break new habits easily to serve my higher purpose. However, when living in an unsupportive environment, it was as easy for me to learn self-sabotaging habits. This was why I had always made sure that I surrounded myself with people and environments that I was able to grow and heal with.

Living in Kuala Lumpur, there was a kind of silent hypnosis that was happening in the backdrop of my consciousness, and these subliminal messages were slowly training my mind to agree with them—and even worse, to live like them! There was a silent social pressure to internalize this narrative, and every day it felt like I was battling some invisible war with my conscience.

I didn't speak up against this narrative; I didn't share my views with anyone for fear that if I did, I would be disappointing and triggering everyone around me. I didn't wish to be ridiculed, to look like a joke for thinking and being different, even if no one said it out loud. The very few times I decided to speak up, I found myself in situations where I confused people more than I inspired them; and I ended up getting weird, awkward stares. Most of the time, I found myself over-explaining my experiences, struggling to find the perfect words.

I constantly felt misunderstood, and the pain of opening myself vulnerably in public social spaces started to eat me up, inside out. This was when my highly sensitive nature turned against me even more. Like watching a horror film or gory movies, the scary images stayed in my mind for a prolonged period of time. Only this time, it was the awkward and blank faces of people that were haunting me.

It's too bad I can't just ignore what's going on.

I still held on to the fear of being judged. This world was not forgiving to those who thought (or were) different. And I knew that humans picked up on the differences of others to cover up their own insecurities about their imperfect authentic selves. Making jokes, gossiping, and denigrating others were coping strategies to direct attention away from their own imperfections. Because of such perceived threats, I hid within myself and kept my stories close to me.

■■
■■

After many months of living in Kuala Lumpur, it seemed as if all the spiritual lessons I'd learned from my time abroad had gone down the drain. I found myself regressing from my spiritual knowing, and the speed of my life started to match the pace of the hustle culture. I found that I unconsciously repressed myself and dumbed myself down to fit in. Avoiding the truth of the matter, I convinced myself that maybe I'd be able to get around this situation in some creative ways. Maybe I could pursue what I believed silently, without anybody knowing, and then put on a different mask when I was interacting with others.

I have to protect myself too!

It sounded like a great idea, but the truth was that this type of thinking stemmed from avoidance and fear. Moreover, it was impossible to do so because my work was all about authentically connecting with people's pain and suffering.

Consequently, an inner conflict started to brew inside me, and I began to hate everything about the city. I started to see the world as a bleak and hopeless place to live.

Besides struggling to adapt to the social aspect of the city, there were so many inconveniences when it came to keeping up the healthy and conscious lifestyle I'd adopted while I was abroad. Most of my basic needs weren't being met now: clean food, air, water; accessibility to holistic health care; and education to feed my personal growth were very much missing. Moreover, not much could be done in a day, because most of my time was spent in a car, stuck in traffic. I certainly didn't want my meaningful life to waste away, idling in a car, and experiencing road rage.

I understood that I wasn't able to compare the situation in a developing country after living with the worldview of a developed country for ten years. Perhaps there were more socioeconomical complexities that I didn't understand, and it was unfair to judge Malaysia with privileged eyes. Furthermore, not accepting my current environment was only creating more suffering for myself. Everything felt like an inconvenience. but that wasn't my main concern.

My main concern was a reality where people were willfully ignorant. They knew they had to change, but most of them turned a blind eye to the truth of the matter.

Why is there little to zero effort from people to move toward a more wholesome paradigm?

I knew that the world was filled with broken systems that didn't serve either the welfare of the people or the natural environment that we lived in. Instead, there were systems applied with insidious intentions that served only the profiteers and those in positions of power. But most of us turned a blind eye to it and lived life as business as usual.

Where are the adults and the elders of the society when I need them to protect us, the children?

Now that I've entered adulthood, why does it seem as if I suddenly have to carry such heavy responsibilities?

I felt completely distraught and went into a deep depression, because I had lost trust in those who were supposed to take care of us. I understood that there were initiatives in the world to resolve these wicked problems that were volatile, uncertain, complex, and ambiguous. However, there were too many of us passively participating in these initiatives. We complained more than doing anything worthwhile to contribute. There were always too many perfect reasons for avoidance that we had all created in our heads:

It isn't our problem to begin with; hence, it isn't our responsibility.

We're too overwhelmed by the intensity of these issues, and we're not able to cope with our personal struggles.

The impact of what we do is too insignificant and unimpactful, so why bother?

We're not professionals, and we're not good enough, so what if we do more damage than good?

There is nothing wrong with the system. Why change? Let's not reinvent the wheel!

Failure after failure, rejection after rejection, have led us to emotional burnout and apathy. What's the point?

Our closest family members and friends don't agree with us, and we don't want to risk damaging our dearest relationships.

And there were more.

I liked to believe that there was inherent goodness in people. The reason why we weren't actively participating in initiatives to make a cleaner and healthier world was not because we were selfish. Instead, it was because we had other commitments that were weighing on our shoulders—we felt we didn't have enough time, energy, attention, or money left to care for something bigger than we were.

My beliefs were confirmed when I shared these very same

concerns with my family and friends. Often their responses were something like, "You can't even stand up on your own two feet, so why are you spending so much effort worrying about worldly problems?"

Partly, I knew that their comments were more about their worldview than about me. However, hearing that made my heart sink. I also knew that they were partially right about where I was in life. I was still struggling to heal from the lower-back incident in Boulder, and my skin health was deteriorating as the days went by. Consequently, I wasn't able to focus on making my own living and was extremely frustrated with my helplessness.

If only I was healthier, then I could show people what I can do!

I had to be concerned about these worldly problems because they impacted me directly. It was the furthest thing from altruism, which had a lot to do with saving the world out of moral responsibility. Instead, my health was at risk. I had to do something about it. I saw the world as a part of me, as I was a part of it. And the health of the world was as significant as my own health. Without the health of the world, I would never be fully at rest, because my health would have been compromised, anyway.

In short, the reason I was concerned was simple: *Because I care!*

My discomfort was never about people not having solutions, but about people giving up too easily from caring for something important to them. Life was precious, but so many took it for granted.

People had lost their love, their light, and their truth. They were living apathetically, purposelessly, and aimlessly.

They were afraid to be fully alive, and their addictions to painkillers and virtual distractions had numbed their souls.

Most of our internal support system with our closest friends and family lacked authentic connections and heartfelt care. We spent so much time fighting about who was right, and too little time caring and bearing witness to each other's common humanity. Our internal support systems had broken down, so all of us continued to psychically numb our emotional awareness and our empathetic capabilities because it seemed too vulnerable to care. Our initial enthusiasm and passion to contribute wholeheartedly with our gifts and talents had faded like dark clouds shrouding our inner rays of hope.

Behind those judgments of mine were fears that one day I would succumb to becoming the by-product of a diseased and apathetic society, just like so many others had. Struggling with this internal conflict, I became uncomfortable in my own skin, in my own home. Furthermore, behind those fears was unresolved pain and hurt from my childhood.

Deep down, I was afraid that I was falling back into the same patterns I had as a child.

As more months passed, I found myself unable to fit into the lifestyle at home. I continually judged the city environment that I was in and habitually complained about it. I became overly self-righteous about what was wrong with the city, and soon enough, I felt disconnected and disheartened, because this was the reality I had to experience daily if I was living at home.

I simply wanted to run away.

I constantly felt that this was not in fact my home, and I needed to search for my home elsewhere. Through a knee-jerk reaction, I continued to go back and forth between other countries even though I knew that wasn't what I needed.

Eventually, this option was no longer available—because in the beginning of 2020, COVID-19 swarmed the world and forced a global lockdown.

This was the very same time when my Saturn-return experience accelerated. The year before the outbreak of COVID-19, many astrologers had come together to speak about this pivotal time that could change the history and timeline of humanity. I was one of the lucky few who had known about it in advance. I wrote an article about it for an astrology magazine and even had a chance to present this topic in front of a group of people. This helped me prepare in advance, but even so, I was completely thrown off by this surprise crisis and was forced to adapt frantically.

What this time meant for me related to credibility and accountability. What I learned over the years of my spiritual journey had to be utilized to adapt to the crisis; otherwise, spirituality was nothing but mere fanciful ideals. I knew that breaking down was a certainty, but whether I made a break-through and a transformation was yet to be determined.

As a consequence of the lockdown, I had to learn to accept where I was in life and strive to make the best out of the situation. There was nowhere to run to. There was no escape but to work though the unfinished love lessons between my home country and me, adapt to the lifestyle and conditions of my family, and most important, lovingly heal myself. The option of going away for another spiritual retreat or relying on my mentors for spiritual advice and healing were instantaneously unavailable.

I was stuck on my own, figuring my own mess out.

During this time, mentors and spiritual teachers whom I had relied heavily upon turned into people who were holding me back from my growth and well-being. It wasn't their fault, but mine to own.

I was desperate to be saved, so I latched on to them and was unknowingly blindsided by their advice. I was completely obsessed with trying to find answers and solutions, and didn't realize that I was asking the wrong questions in the first place. I was so entrenched in my victimhood mentality that I was never able to see myself as the solution.

I wasn't able to trust my own choices and decisions, which left me feeling completely disempowered. I knew so many things intellectually, but I was incapacitated emotionally and spiritually. When left to my own devices, I behaved like a child who clung on to a life jacket that wasn't helping him swim on his own. Hence, the Universe took all my life jackets away from me, throwing me into the deep end of the sea.

My lower-back pain wasn't healing. The chronic atopic dermatitis that I'd carried with me since I was eight years old started to flare up out of nowhere and raged out of control. Life became more intense all around, and I had to confront the pain of both my body and my soul. I was becoming more depressed as the days passed. Meaninglessness infected me as dark clouds of despair loomed over me, forcing me to shut myself in further.

I was in a downward spiral.

This made me think about the pain of the past and how it was different from the pain of the present. This time, I was truly exhausted, and my willpower was broken.

I started to develop signs of chronic fatigue syndrome, and no matter how much sleep I got, I wasn't rested. The nights were long, and the days were numbing. I felt like the living dead. The prolonged national lockdown wasn't very helpful, either. I was out of touch with nature, stuck in a concrete jungle, and regularly numbing myself with Netflix and addictively paying for perks in online games. Suicidal thoughts started to invade my consciousness as I saw both the future of my life and the future of humanity becoming so bleak and so stale.

Thus, thoughts of ending my life were very tempting.

"I tried my best, didn't I?" I questioned the Universe with a passive-aggressive demeanor.

I thought that if I had tried my best in my life, then I was entitled to give up that life. I thought it was an easy way out. The high-rise condominium that I was living in made it even easier. The windows weren't protected, and they were big enough for anyone to jump out of.

And that was precisely the problem.

It was so easy that I felt insulted.

CHAPTER FIFTEEN

The Choice of No Return

The COVID-19 lockdown of 2020 was not the first time I had experienced nihilistic thoughts. I had been through worse situations and had experienced more intense despair before.

Why did I want to give up now, when I didn't just give up then?

In the middle of 2007, I returned to Malaysia from a failed venture to study in Australia. I didn't complete my studies because my health had deteriorated and my body was a living hell. I wasn't very kind to myself in this situation, either. I was disappointed and resented my inability to be resilient. I thought that being unhealthy was a poor reason.

I damned myself further by attacking my self-worth. My inner self-talk was toxic. I viewed myself as irredeemable, not worthy of love, and completely and utterly useless. My inner

turmoil stemming from this failure left me shaking involuntarily from a cold chill coming from within. I thought that
maybe I didn't deserve to live, simply because I failed.

The rage that resulted from my failure was vengeful, and
my inner being was filled with despair and hate. There was a
centrifugal whirlpool of destructive emotions that plummeted
me to the bottom of the ocean floor as it capsized my lifeboat
of false optimism. This was the very first time that I understand the true depths of truly dark emotions. Prior to this, I'd
had no idea that I was capable of experiencing such darkness
within me. It was so addictive that the shadows lingering within the darkness of my emotions were waiting eagerly for me to
turn into one of them.

Being physically feeble and emotionally vulnerable, I didn't
have the strength to fight these emotions. I allowed the darkness to envelop me like an ameba engulfing its prey. Internally,
I felt permanently disfigured by the ugliness of life, and my
pride disintegrated into nothingness. I became numb, adopting a stone-cold outlook as the life from my eyes dimmed. The
colors in my life turned gray as I contemplated the mad world
I was living in, and I became an apathetic member of the living
dead. At the same time, my sense of "I" melted away, and a
beast burning with rage and vengeance awakened within me.
It had been waiting to take over, and now the opportunity
had come.

*Why had I made the decision to study in Australia in the
first place?*

Well, I thought I had done so because I wanted to be like
all my other cool friends. I believed that the educational system in my country wasn't good enough for me, and I had to
prove myself in an environment that had higher standards.

I was too ignorant and too proud, which led me to almost throw my life away: I'd lost my first teenage love to a long-distance relationship that never worked out; I'd lost my health to another big flare-up on my skin; I was ashamed of coming home after being all high and mighty by pursuing academics outside of my country; and consequently, I'd lost my confidence and sanity to anguish and deep grief.

Time slowed down within these painful emotions. My life flashed before my seventeen-year-old eyes. I was being asked to look back to determine whether I had lived a meaningful life. I watched my life crumble away, like fine china falling to the floor in slow motion, soon to be shattered into a million fine pieces. I was being pushed off the edge of a cliff, and there was no turning back. I had a taste of what it felt like to make a choice of no return.

Sink or swim. Fall into the abyss or learn how to fly. Clean up those pieces of china or turn them into a new mosaic art piece. Continue to wallow in self-pity or take up the responsibility to take charge of my own life.

The choice was mine to make.

A few months after returning home from Australia, I had enough of the pharmaceutical quick fix for my autoimmune condition. I set my heart and soul willfully on eliminating any Western medication, drew a boundary with respect to ingesting any unnatural substances from food and drink, and threw all chemical mixtures and toxicity out of my life.

My exact rationale was: *Anything that kills nature kills me.* It was a difficult decision to make, but I had to be radical and decisive.

I was trapped in a situation where I didn't know who to approach for sensible health advice. The doctors I had seen in the past had promised me that medication was the way to go, but that had not worked out well for me. The raging beast within me now shouted at me to get rid of the medication—without hesitation—so I took a cupboard full of it, dumped it all in the trash, and made sure it never got back into my life again. I had to do my research on my own. No longer was I able to rely on professionals or adults to determine what was best for me.

They had all failed me.

As is the case with any prolonged usage of drugs, there were side-effect reactions when I stopped taking my medication so suddenly, and it didn't take long for them to kick in. Maybe you have seen in TV and movies what it looks like when someone "goes cold turkey," and that's what happened to me. The rehabilitation process involved in ceasing the use of immunosuppressant pharmaceutical drugs such as corticosteroids was not pleasant at all.

No one talked about this back then, and there was no social media on which to share my experience about what I might expect from withdrawal. I was completely in the dark, and only more than a decade later did I find out that this condition is called *topical steroid withdrawal.*

At that time, no one had any idea that this condition was *iatrogenic,* meaning that it was an illness caused by medical treatments or pharmaceutical drugs. As a consequence, I spent many moments in my healing journey being criticized by others for stopping my medication. However, not knowing where that iron will of resolution came from, I paid no heed to that noise. I steeled myself to go through the entire withdrawal journey, following my inner voice, which was my only way to maintain my sanity.

Contrary to what I looked like on the outside, the withdrawal effect wasn't the problem, but the beginning of healing. My body's innate wisdom in its quest to dispel toxins through my skin was activated. The opportunity for the raging beast within me to be free had finally come. It was here to rebel; to protest; to express the rage, discord, and injustice that it had been experiencing. Freeing the beast from sedative pharmaceutical drugs had invited my body to fully express itself without any need to hold back.

After a couple of weeks being medication-free, the itching was beyond my control, and I was scratching myself repeatedly. My entire body was covered in flaky skin that was full of scabs, and it was so inflamed that I looked like a burn victim. The scratched-up wounds weren't healing normally, and the scabs piled up one on top of the other, making my skin look so deformed that I appeared to be a poorly made wax mannequin. The itching was so intense that it took over all sensations in my body, and along with the pain from the scratching, there were no restful days where I could escape my excruciating mental battle. The only natural response to satisfy the itch was to scratch that flaky skin even more.

The nefarious thing about the itching was that no matter how I dealt with it, it was never satisfied. Once the scratching had begun, the itching amplified, and as a result, the scratching had to intensify. In moments when I had no control over the scratching, I was completely dissociative. Open wounds or not, I *had* to scratch. It became a vicious cycle that only stopped when I had no more energy left.

Day after day, it was rinse and repeat. I had to learn how to alleviate my itching without scratching. I used sheer will-power, mental fortitude, and awareness of my breath to try to get me through it. Nevertheless, no matter how much will-power or mental fortitude I mustered, at some point, I eventually gave in to the itching. It felt like my body had gone into self-destruct mode on purpose just to restore itself, destroying any falsity and inauthenticity that was attached to my being. The thick masks of social imprints slowly got chipped away violently, as the raging sculptor from my subconscious began constructing its masterpiece from all the past anguish and despair. No matter how much I fought, darkness always triumphed over me.

However, I wasn't entirely alone in this battle. At the beginning of my hellish days of recovery, I was introduced to a traditional Chinese medicine practitioner who promised revolutionary methods to reverse my skin disorder naturally. I revised my diet right away, as I was given an education about the atrocious food industry. I learned that most food—be it meat or produce—was contaminated with pharmaceutical antibiotics and hormones, insecticides, chemical agents, and pollutants. In "safe" amounts and in the short term, these agents didn't cause symptoms, as our bodies were able to naturally detoxify and rebalance themselves. Nonetheless, no one talked about what happened when these toxins accumulated within the body.

As explained by this practitioner, my body was slow to detoxify and had a poor capacity to return to balance. If its ability to process the toxins was overloaded, any additional toxins had to be moved toward the skin, which caused it to flare up. Since the skin is the biggest organ of the body, this was the quickest way to expel the toxins. Looking at my body in this perspective gave me a new appreciation for its natural intelligence to heal.

Why have I never met a doctor who talked about this until now?

The next suggestion for treatment was to do blood-cupping therapy to cleanse my body of toxins. This involved pricking my skin with fine needles to induce bleeding, and then sucking the blood out of a vacuum suction cup. The blood that was released was usually stale, murky, and sticky, with a foul odor, which were signs of the presence of toxins. This treatment worked well in reducing my itch. However, the very same treatment created more inflammation and more aggressive responses from my immune system.

At the same time, I received acupuncture to restore the energy of my body and induce natural healing to take place. In addition, I was given herbal medicine to soak in to heal the wounds from the needles and to reduce the itching. The bath also helped remove the shedding of my skin more easily, and soothed the renewal process involved in growing new skin cells.

My mistake was that I thought I had to endure pain in order to heal. These treatment methods were met with the utmost skepticism from my father. The truth was that I was horrified by the whole process myself. It was too extreme to comprehend, yet the relentless voice that resided deep within my heart nudged me to proceed, anyway. So I put on a brave face and became a master of enduring pain.

It was the only choice—and the best option I had. I knew that I was in for the long haul, and I had nothing behind me to turn back to. I was also blind to any possible future. It was a desperate moment, and I was willing to take a chance on any glimmer of light to move forward.

I have already lost everything. How bad could this be?

I could only take this leap of faith. With my undying will to heal and the desperation for a magical reset button, I went through a period of life that was unthinkable and unimaginable. And I thought, *How did a simple, naïve desire to go to Australia lead me to this situation?*

⸭

The torment intensified a week after my first treatment. As I was preparing for an herbal bath, the sensation of itching heightened beyond my means to hold myself back. Like the transformation of a werewolf in the middle of the night of a full moon, I suddenly felt as if I had shape-shifted claws to tear myself open and remove all the impurities I had internalized my entire life. The burning hatred enveloped my hands, and in a manic state, I deconstructed and disfigured myself by scratching away layers of my outermost epidermis.

It didn't matter if I was bleeding.

It didn't matter if there was pain.

The raging beast kept going, even as I was still willfully fighting back to prevent damage to my skin. My dimly lit conscious self knew that if that manic scratching continued, the recovery journey ahead would be much longer.

Like a wax figurine, the congregated skin cells from the top of my head to the bottom of my body were soft and scaly.

My body felt fermented and rotten. The odor of the toxic lymph fluid that started to ooze out of my skin was unnaturally astringent. Chemical wastes were forcefully removed. My body started to disperse immense heat that was able to be felt if someone was a foot away from my body. My inflammation went into overdrive, and it felt like I was being burned alive by acid.

And yet, my hands didn't stop, the bleeding didn't stop, the oozing of the foul-smelling lymph fluid didn't stop, the itch didn't stop, and the pain didn't stop. The only thing that stopped was time. I got stuck in a loop of eternal sorrow.

I was completely dissociated. My entire nervous system froze.

The next thing I knew, I started to burst into tears of anguish and screamed at the top of my lungs in shock. Despite the immense heat that was emanating from my body, I was frozen in a crouching position, stark naked, while shaking and trembling in fear.

"What have I done? What have I done? What have I done? What have I done? What have I done? What have I done? What have I done? What have I done? What have I done? WHAT HAVE I DONE?" I chanted on repeat.

My consciousness was immediately fractured by the intensity of the experience. I regressed quickly from a human being to an animal that only knew fear. It was primal, and my struggle to survive and soothe my pain was instinctual as the intense shaking continued.

The only person who came to my aid at that time was my mother. She was dumbfounded by the state I was in and was clueless as to what she needed to do to ease my suffering. She wasn't able to touch me, as the burning of my skin was similar to a third-degree burn. It was a condition for which I needed to be hospitalized, and it was beyond common sense that I refused to go to the hospital.

The mother's instinct to protect, to soothe, and to care was activated right way. She knew she had to put my needs before hers. Despite not knowing what to do, her instinct told her to show up with maternal compassion. Hence, she just ended up holding space for me, gently asking me what I needed from her.

What would you do as a parent if all you could do was bear witness?

If there was absolutely nothing you could do?

If you had to open your heart completely to the truth of the moment?

There was no fixing me. There was no trying to make me feel better. There was absolutely nothing but simply witnessing the arguably divine unfoldment of my body's healing process.

The floor was filled with blood, sweat, toxic lymph fluid, tears, piles of scattered skin scabs, as well as stains bearing the evidence of the complete hopelessness of my emotional torment. Eventually, my mother slowly and encouragingly walked me into an herbal bath she'd prepared.

Getting into the bathtub was difficult, as my entire body was an open wound. Getting out of the bath was similarly difficult, as I no longer had a protective layer. I felt raw and unprotected. The wisdom of my body responded by oozing more of the lymph fluid out of the layers of my skin; and finally, when the layer was covered, it hardened up to form a temporary and poorly constructed layer of skin for protection.

I was like a caterpillar that had disintegrated itself into the form of a cocoon. There were no promises that the transformation into a butterfly was possible. Recovery felt impossible. I was forced into a situation where I had no choice but to be courageous enough to accept what was. It was an unwilling trust and an optionless faith. I didn't feel particularly connected to any religion or deity, but in that moment, all I wanted was God's embrace.

Where is Divine Grace while all this is happening?

Maybe this is what death feels like.

Maybe I don't need to resist anymore.

Maybe all I need to do is surrender my life to the hands of the Universe.

Maybe I just have to stop trying, and simply show up.

I felt like a broken soldier who was no longer useful on the battlefield. I had to resign and give up the fight, recognizing that the inner battle of healing had only just begun. This healing process turned out to be completely different from what I expected. The enemy wasn't anything out there; it had nothing to do with my decision to go to Australia, or the fact that I had failed and screwed up my life. This battle wasn't even related to the disease, but rather, it had to do with how I felt about myself.

Once I was wounded, the scars were permanent. As much as I would love to delete these memories as if they never happened, the gruesome images and the chilling sensations of this incident successfully embedded themselves into my cellular memory. I was so vulnerable and broken that at any moment I could have gone into psychosis. That experience made the notion of death seem trivial. Healing from this trauma became my sole battle.

After the bath, I made my way to my bed, wearing very little clothing and with only a thin blanket to keep myself warm.

What was real and what was imaginary seemed to blur. Not able to move much anymore, I soothed myself while silently chanting the mantra *Om Mani Padme Hum* in my mind over and over.

And just like that, I drifted into a restless sleep.

Maybe it's better for me if I don't wake up after this.

I did wake up, though. As soon as I did, my father was by my side. I wasn't able to move my body, as the skin had started to harden, and the pain was excruciating. Seeing a son who was in such a state of distress must have left a traumatic mark on him.

What was going through both of my parents' minds was beyond my knowing. I was only able to assume that guilt and shame were weighing down upon their shoulders. Perhaps there was a narrative about not doing enough to protect their child from such suffering.

My dad's gut was fired up. He had to do something. He had to fix this problem right away. Yet there was nothing to be done.

I wondered how hopeless he must have felt confronting the reality that he wasn't able to do anything for his child. The despair must have been overwhelming.

After a long moment of silence, he gathered his courage and whispered to me, "Would you be willing to go to the hospital? Let me take you there and get you out of this crisis."

"No," I replied meekly. It was simple, clear, and direct.

In that moment, I was an unrecognizable child of his. Meanwhile, what was emerging was the presence of an intelligence deeper than who I thought I was. I was no longer his child. He was no longer my parent. I was just a being whose soul was emerging. I was still operating with a fractured consciousness from the shock. Despite that, my consciousness was as clear as day.

"I want to see it through to the end of this treatment. I believe that I will recover and heal eventually. Can you please return the authority of my health and my body back to me? I just need you to believe in me and trust me," I said as my resolve sharpened.

I can't know what my father felt upon hearing these words from his son. I only knew that he gave in to me, in defeat yet with respect. And in the kindest, most sincere, and heartfelt voice, he whispered, "Yes, I trust you and believe in you. I'm proud of you for being so brave."

His response was the greatest gift my father could have given me. They were the perfect words I needed to hear to get through my healing crisis.

Perhaps all I wanted from him was for him to trust and believe in me. In receiving those words, this crisis had turned into an unexpected opportunity to heal something deeper, a healing of the relationship between a father and a son. It wouldn't have happened if everything was business as usual. That incident initiated my never-ending search for truth—the truth to be a holistic, healthy human being who had the capacity to express his entelechy in this seemingly complex world.

CHAPTER SIXTEEN

Birth of the Name *Chiron*

There has never been a dull moment in my life ever since that incident in 2007. It was the greatest turning point of my life, and led me into a never-ending healing journey.

Where is the Universe leading me, anyway?

The strangest thing of all was that, after all the attempts at healing I had made, I assumed that once it actually happened, I would be able to go back to my old life. But that was never the case.

When will I finally be done with this?

Now, the collective hopelessness in the air of 2020 matched my own. As the lockdown extended longer than we would have liked, more stories of chaos and emotional turbulence started to surface. Upon hearing these accounts—the lack of personal space at home, the disconnection from natural elements, people's complaints and negative thoughts, and the propensity to develop an addiction to the internet—my hypersensitive bodily system went crazy.

I didn't need to go online to feel the chaos of the collective consciousness, and every day I had to confront and battle my inner psyche just to find some semblance of sanity. Furthermore, living in a high-rise condominium definitely didn't help, as I was so far away from the earth and couldn't ground and discharge all the mental and emotional energies that were streaming into my being. The built-up stress in my system without a discharge was leading me toward a deterioration of my health. Being in distress became my default mode, and I could not turn it off.

Despite all that, what this time gave me was a lot of space to look at my entire life. From taking a huge risk to stop medication in 2007 and recovering from the withdrawal; to taking a leap of faith to leave prestigious universities twice in 2012 and 2013, respectively, just to figure out my life path; to showing up faithfully in the land where American dreams are made in 2014 to begin my spiritual training; to following the tug of my heart and my gut to the middle of a rainforest in Peru in 2017, just to meet the mysterious white lions of Timbavati and understand nature's law of love and respect in 2018; and then, to have come back home to Malaysia, just to be stuck in a COVID-19 lockdown situation—I realized that there was a bigger, more invisible thread going on behind the scenes.

My healing journey was certainly not an ordinary one, and it had taken me on a ride to self-actualization. Following the thread of my own story, this moment was also leading me into something beyond what my intellect could comprehend.

One morning I muttered to myself, "This chapter of my life must not end like this!"

I have had enough of feeling so helpless, but what can I do to change my fate right now?

Invasive thoughts of self-harm attacked my mind each day. Soon, it became a voice that I was indifferent to as I determined to maintain my sanity through my meditation practices. I convinced myself not to believe those thoughts by repeating a mantra in my head:

I am not my thoughts. I am not my body. I am who I am.
I am not my thoughts. I am not my body. I am who I am.
I am not my thoughts. I am not my body. I am who I am.

I hoped that if I at least didn't give these thoughts the power to control my mind or my life, maybe one day they would disappear on their own. However, this hope was about as good as a Band-Aid as far as combatting those invasive thoughts. I knew that this half-hearted solution wasn't going to lead me anywhere.

My skin's inflammation was not calming down, despite all my efforts to diet, fast, and experiment with various ways of biohacking. My sleep was also suffering because the itch was most intense at night, which kept me awake. This led my circadian rhythms to break down, so I was sleeping during the day and was wide awake at night. The mental chatter and emotional turmoil persisted, and my vitality was diminishing.

Besides that, my lower-back injury started to worsen as it

continued to perpetuate more pain, preventing me from doing any proper exercise. In fact, it was so bad that I had to crawl out of bed every morning. It had been a year since I had initially felt excruciating back pain in Boulder, and my lack of recovery made me think that I would have to live with this condition my entire life. For a movement enthusiast and a dancer, this was a huge blow to my soul.

Despite all my suffering, the only thing that looked hopeful to me was the clear and clean air that had previously been a rare occurrence in Kuala Lumpur. Nature was healing when human activities stopped. I thought that was something positive that was coming out of this dreadful time.

I avoided speaking to anybody about my condition and my experiences. I didn't want to trouble anyone, adding to the stresses of the world that had already been imposed on them unwillingly.

Furthermore, I was already in a lucky position, because in that moment, I didn't have to work and was able to rely on my family to get myself back together. I knew there were people out there who were suffering and in much worse situations. At least I had some tools I was able to use in order to try and heal.

Nevertheless, despite all the mental and emotional fortitude I tried to bolster myself with, the lack of actual conversations, honest perspectives, and safe open space to share what I was going through plummeted me deeper into my neurosis.

I was feeling more trapped than ever.

If chanting a mantra didn't work, I reasoned with myself that I had to try a completely different method. And this was the moment that I thought about my conversation with the Universe back in Encinitas.

If I can't run away from my mind or make it go away, maybe I should go toward it. Perhaps I can try to be a Milarepa again.

Hence, I continued to entertain thoughts of ending my life.

If I die right now, will I have any regrets?

Will people finally think about me and love me after I die?

Will my absence inspire the people around me to appreciate life more?

Why do people have to wait for the last moments of life before they decide to love one another?

What is the meaning of my life?

In those moments when I contemplated my own death, what convinced me more than anything else to stay alive, was, strangely enough, the irritation of not completing a task.

Over the years, I had developed the rigidity of a taskmaster. Everything needed to be planned out accordingly, and I disliked moments when my plans were interrupted. Such behavior had seeped through during my academic life, progressed into my professional life, and had finally become a part of my mundane living. I disliked watching a movie halfway through, no matter how bad it was. I *had* to finish it. I didn't enjoy multitasking when doing my house chores because I ended up wasting more time. When something was left undone, a mental splinter emerged at the back of my head that subsequently made me feel like something was missing. I needed things to be done!

Similarly, thinking about dying made me feel like I was missing the point of life. The introspection of considering the worst-case scenario helped me gain the perspective that my life was just like watching an unfinished movie.

I was the protagonist. If I was able to watch the protagonist, then that made me the director of my movie. And if I was the director, then I had the power to write the next episode of my life. I didn't have control over my circumstances, but I definitely had the power to choose how I wanted to experience my life.

There was a choice here: *to wallow in my pain miserably, or celebrate my pain lovingly.*

Instead of running away from my pain, I started moving toward it, curiously exploring how far into my pain I was able to enter viscerally. I started being inquisitive about my pain, and that made me less numb. With that, there was more space in my body, and that helped me feel again. I realized that this made me completely human. From such a radical acceptance came an inner knowing that in that moment of turbulence, my soul was being forged into a diamond through the pressure of the pain.

I remembered that the Universe was always kind. It never gave me any challenges that were beyond my capabilities, even if that was how it seemed from my victimized perspective. I concluded that if the Universe had put me in such a difficult situation, then it must have had a high regard for me. The Universe was expecting me to make a breakthrough.

Slowly, I started to recognize that I was equipped with more than enough life skills, emotional intelligence, and spiritual wisdom to work through my situation. As such, I made a deeper resolution and commitment to myself to see through what was next. I reasoned that if I was able to experience such despair, then I would be able to move through *anything* in life, just like I had experienced the effects of drug withdrawal in 2007. In my darkest moments, I found that love from the Universe was very present.

How have I not experienced this before?

Maybe my awareness had simply not been present enough to receive it. Love was never able to be present because I was too busy seeing through the eyes of the victim and wallowing in my misery.

I took the first step by picking up a pen to write. Journaling and freewriting were two of the rituals I had adopted before to access greater consciousness beyond the victimized part of me. Further contemplation in my head was useless if I kept seeing my situation from the eyes of a victim.

By writing whatever came through my stream of consciousness without any judgment, I was able to explore a higher perspective. Out of this heightened perspective, I was able to go beyond the tunnel vision of the victim to create new meaning from my pain. This was the most effective way for me to communicate with the Universe.

"What is the good here that I'm not seeing?" I asked, hoping to re-create those sentimental moments when I had enlightening conversations with the Universe. I was in a dire situation, desperate for some glimpse of light at the end of this tunnel—hopefully sooner rather than later.

I need some sort of divine guidance right away.

Without any attachment to an answer, I wrote whatever came through, and within the freewriting process, I was reminded of the three sacred questions that I had learned from my nature-connected life-coach training.

What do I notice?

What does it mean?

What is it teaching me?

These questions helped me be nonjudgmental with respect to the self-inquiry process. Little did I know, I was actually doing therapy with myself.

Most of what I wrote was about how free I felt when I traveled in search of discovering who I was out in the world. Oddly enough, being anonymous and immersed in the culture of others were the moments when I felt most comfortable in my own skin. Maybe this was because when no one knew who I was, there was an opportunity for me to simply be my ordinary self. There were no expectations of how I was *supposed* to behave or how I had to present myself in front of others.

I just had to be me.

I remembered that there were people in my life who were able to accept who I was and reciprocated such love. They were able to see me in the light of my highest potential that I had no awareness about. They believed in me unconditionally. That gave me a special sense of belonging, which inspired me to call them my *soul family*. They spoke the same spiritual language that I did, and they shared the same path to heal and self-actualize with a motivation that wasn't just out of the love for oneself, but for the collective.

I remembered a stranger who once attended the same nature-connected coaching workshop with me. She looked me in the eyes and simply said, "You are needed in the world!" That earnest sharing was powerful enough for me to move through anything.

Recognizing how meaningful this was, I wanted to be part of the co-creation of a new human paradigm too. We were all learning how to move through the complexity of the world with fierce love. The great news was that I was able to find this community of people from place to place. However, despite all that great synergy and bonding, these relationships were all short-lived because we all came from different locations on the planet.

My soul family gave me a sense of belonging on Earth that was difficult to forget. I thought it was an essential need for me to thrive. Despite all this idealistic dreaming, at the end of the day, I was confronted by these questions:

Why is all of this not possible when I'm at home?

What is my resistance?

Am I just not a good fit for this place?

How can that be? This is my birthplace!

Am I simply an outcast in my own country and in my own family?

As I continued to dive deeper into the self-inquiry process, I was reminded of the term *transitional character*, which was coined by psychologist and author Carlfred Broderick. The transitional character was the one who, in a single generation of a family, changed the entire course of the lineage. In my case, I also had the ambitious desire to change the entire course of my country's awareness toward health and healing. I wanted to make a huge impact in my own way, because that was what it meant to live a meaningful life.

And more than anything, I believed that my entelechy was made to do so. That was my human design. How it was going to be done was a mystery for me to find out.

Understanding the transitional character made me see myself in a new light. I wasn't simply rebellious, righteous, and resentful about my birth city's environment for the sake of it. My soul was figuring out the way to metabolize all the poisonous and destructive behaviors that were being passed down from my predecessors, both of my family and my country.

Despite the great intentions of my soul, I also knew that being rebellious, righteous, and resentful were not the most skillful and effective ways to confront the truth of the matter. Beneath all the rage, grief, shame, guilt, and hunger, I desired a future that was radically different from my childhood, especially for those who came after me. I wanted to tear up the systemic trauma and build a new foundation that was rooted in love, rather than coming from a place of fear disguised as love. Thinking about the latter was too sickening and toxic to bear.

This means that I have to keep on living for the sake of it.

At that moment of discovering new meaning out of pain and suffering, a pristine and precious memory from the back of my consciousness started to glimmer. I whispered, "Ah, maybe this was why the name *Chiron* came into my life."

Chiron was the name of the Greek god who famously carried the mantle "the wounded healer." In mythological and astrological studies, Chiron was an archetype who represented a part of our wounded psyche that came with many great gifts. For some ineffable reason, I had a close connection with him. There was nothing cool or amazing to be named after someone who was wounded his entire life. Yet I chose it anyway.

Why am I so adamant about being a wounded healer?

Is it out of a spiritual and egoistic attachment to my pain and suffering, because that was what defined my identity for my entire life up till now?

Or is it out of the hope that in embodying this archetype, I'm able to transcend my pain and suffering and finally live in the world with well-being, peace, and harmony?

Maybe the memory of how I got the name *Chiron* in the first place could reveal some insights for me.

In 2015, I was deep in the wilderness, surrounded by the Sequoioideae. I called them "the gentle giants of the redwood forest." They were famous for being the largest and tallest trees in the world. Their postures were magnificent and ancient and sublime. They reminded me of how old and resilient nature has always been, and how the spirit of nature radiates with aliveness. The skyscrapers of the city had never matched this magnitude of magnificence in comparison. Human inventions and creations always fell short in contrast with the natural intelligence of Life.

Sure, skyscrapers of the modern century have surpassed the height of these ancient trees, but will they be able to last as long as these trees?

These trees were very much alive. I felt that they were watching and witnessing my every childlike movement. I was treading upon their land awkwardly, with doubt and suspicion, but I was simultaneously mesmerized by their presence.

I had never been alone in the wild before. I had camped in nature, but that was mostly in public parks and gardens, which were all within the confines of human control. For a lifetime city boy who'd spent most of his time in a convenient and enclosed concrete jungle, being in a rugged forest with no fixed terrain was beyond my comfort zone.

I was on my first vision quest ever, and I was both nervous and excited. I was anticipating the next unfoldment of my self-discovery, hoping that it would bring me closer to my entelechy.

I had come with the intention of demystifying my fears and limiting narratives about the wild; and in the process, I hoped to rediscover the wildness within me. I'd been disconnected from the wildness of nature for the longest time, and my soul yearned to quench its thirst by remembering the wonder and ordinary magic within me.

Also, I had simply followed the green light that both my heart and my gut feeling had given me. I knew it was the intelligence within me, guiding me home to who I truly was.

Hence, I was drawn to a vision quest. I heard that it was a rite of passage to remember the truth of our nature, practiced by Native Americans to initiate the young into adulthood and to receive their life's calling. Being lost in the world appealed to me.

The first time I heard about such a concept, I convinced myself that if only there had been elders in my own Malaysian community who could have been able to guide me to my truth, then I wouldn't have had to go through so much pain, or go so far in the world just to have an opportunity for this experience. As a result, I felt bitter and angry. I was mad at my predecessors, who had given me everything but proper guidance in this disorienting world.

I had no idea if the vision quest I was about to participate in was true to the original culture and intention. Yet I knew it was what I needed at this stage of my spiritual maturity.

I came in with the intention of searching for a name or an identity that would befit me in this world. I felt that the old identity I'd been carrying around wasn't functional or authentic. I believed that a part of me needed to die so that a new part of me could be reborn. I needed to know my path forward in a world of darkness. I wasn't seeking to run away from who I was, but I needed to know that within all the darkness of the human experience, there existed a brighter light and a greater purpose.

I was told that whatever happened in an initiation ritual carried with it a level of unexpectedness and uncertainty, where moments of time and space of past, present, and future were distorted, but which might lead to moments of infinite possibilities. In the sit spot that I found in the wilderness, I dropped into an altered state of consciousness where infinite possibilities showed up.

Behind the scenes, the community of the Sequoioideae was bearing witness for me. For the very first time, I had a different sense of what it felt like to be home. In the city, home had to do with accessibility to all sorts of conveniences. That accessibility came with the price of psychic disconnection, of feeling uprooted and alienated, even with respect to my closest relationships.

However, as I lay down in the middle of nowhere, with no one around, along with the absence of the usual conveniences, this home in nature offered me an experience of what it meant to feel deeply connected to the interconnectedness of this world. I felt welcomed, witnessed, and was completely at ease in the intuitive wisdom of my being.

There was something ineffable about being in nature for a prolonged period of time while fasting. I had the mystical experience of observing myself, teaching myself, and guiding myself to my personal truth. There was a sense of knowing even amid the thoughts that were surfacing.

Intermingled in rhythms of arousal and quiescence, my consciousness dropped in and out of old memories where old wounds and injuries emerged. Most of them were repressed, strong emotions. Unfortunately, I had to experience this intensity within my body. While being submerged in my deep appreciation for the wonder and ordinary magic of nature, I was also immersed in pain, fired from the pain receptors of my lower back. It was a mystery to me as to how this was happening to me—I was in good shape, and had not been dealing with any physical trauma in this part of my body prior to the vision quest. Yet the energy from the bottom of my spine was rising, and I was overcome by pain and confusion. My skin, which had been calm before the vision quest, began to set itself on fire, and the inflammation spiraled out of control.

Amid the intensity of the pain, I had a flashback of many of the painful moments in my life. They were mostly about how I felt unrecognized, with many of my emotional needs being unmet when I was a child. They were also about how unfortunate I had been to develop chronic atopic dermatitis, which no one had an answer to.

The way I had dealt with it until now was to try to push it away and pay it no attention. I was afraid of being weak, so I simply moved on with life and bypassed my human vulnerability. I had no respect for my energy, and I saw my body as a blind horse who only knew to dash forward. Burnout was inevitable. Clearly, there was no one to blame for it, not even myself, as I had only been a young adolescent.

As my consciousness deepened, I accessed memories that were beyond this life. There was a faint familiarity of being a wounded soldier who wanted to give up his life, but his undying will didn't allow him to do so. There was also a moment of claircognizance, where I knew that once upon a time, I had been rejected, punished, and burned at the stake by a spiritual authority for my imperfections. Back then, I had suffered the existential guilt of my "wrongness" so that even an ever-loving God had forsaken me.

As these painful experiences entered a threshold, I wondered how old I was as a soul and how long I had endured my journey just to discover who I was. Then, going beyond space and time, I recalled the myth of the centaur Chiron. I noticed how similar his story was to mine, symbolically.

Chiron's mythology began with the rejection of his existence. That was his first wound. He was abandoned out of shame and disgust by his parents—Cronus, a god; and Philyra, a water nymph—for being born as a monstrosity. He was a hybrid, which meant that he was half-mortal and half-immortal, while his appearance was half-human and half-horse.

In Greek mythology, centaurs are notorious for their crude and barbaric behavior; but Chiron, in contrast, was intelligent, civilized, skilled, and kind as a result of the parentage of his foster parents: Apollo and his twin sister, Artemis. They taught him all about medicine, music, archery, martial arts, hunting, astrology, and prophecy, and this knowledge made him rise above all the other centaurs. Despite rejection, and his poor reputation as a centaur, Chiron overcame the stigma of his appearance and was judged by the quality of his character, making him a maverick among his kind. Eventually, he became a notable mentor to Greek heroes such as Hercules, Achilles, Perseus, and many more.

His second wound was exposed when he was shot accidentally by a poison arrow that Hercules had released from his bow. It was the very same poison that Chiron had given to Hercules when he was under Chiron's mentorship. The irony was that not only had he been shot by his own student, but he was poisoned by his own instructions. This led him on a journey to seek medicine and healing despite already being a master healer. Sadly, Chiron was unsuccessful, doomed to live a life of pain and agony. He wasn't able to die because he was an immortal. As talented as he was, this wound made him dysfunctional and vulnerable.

An opportunity showed up for Chiron when he bargained to surrender his immortality and die in exchange for the freedom of Prometheus, who had been punished for stealing the divine fire he had given humanity in the form of knowledge and technology. This enraged Zeus, and Prometheus was sentenced to eternal death by having an eagle rip his liver out every day; however, Prometheus's immortality allowed his liver to be continually regenerated. Rather than hanging on to this godhood and his immortality, Chiron chose to exchange his life to free Prometheus from his eternal pain. Again, he had proven the nobility of his loving-kindness. Touched by his actions, Zeus, who commanded the heavens, shot his lightning bolt to resurrect Chiron from the depths of the underworld into the stars in the sky to be honored as the constellation *Centaurus*.

I had always found myths fascinating because they allowed me to imagine possibilities beyond what I thought I knew. Myths had been how ancient peoples found guidance when they were lost and stuck in their ways. The creation fables, the heroic legends, and the fairy tales were much more than literal bedtime stories. Within them, there were lessons intended to invoke the human psyche with creativity to go beyond the known.

Likewise, I found the myth of Chiron to be connected to the story of my own. Perhaps I had to find my way out, in the same way that Chiron had found his way out of eternal pain and agony.

Chiron could have blamed his parents for not loving him unconditionally.

Chiron could have wallowed in misery and victimhood and not learned any skills from Apollo and Artemis.

Chiron could have blamed Hercules and used his position as a mentor to narcissistically control him for what he'd done.

Chiron could have given up looking for cures and medicine.

Chiron could have remained egoistical and prideful in order to keep his immortality.

Instead, Chiron had done none of this. He maintained the path of loving-kindness, honor, and humility, and was a true student of life. He wasn't self-righteous, but rather, took responsibility for his actions, his deeds, and his fate. A god that was willing to surrender his immortality was a being who dedicated his whole life to getting to the heart of the matter. This was what it took to understand true healing.

Through understanding his mythology, I came to know that Chiron was the true mentor spirit for me. As such, I made a commitment to take the name *Chiron* to help light my path forward. This moment of cathartic pain turned into an ecstatic experience for me. I'd received a divine message from nature, and a vision to understand the nature of pain, while discovering health and healing along the way. It wasn't about succumbing to the victimhood or martyrdom of being a healer. Rather, it was a dedication to embody the truth of healing and well-being.

As time and space went back to normal, drums were beaten from afar to call for a return from the vision quest. The pain of my lower back didn't ease up, so I was pretty sure I wouldn't be able to walk back. As I tried to stand up, two caterpillars showed themselves to me by dancing with one another, curling into each other to form a double-helix shape. Wonder and ordinary magic were very much alive. I felt my inner willpower renewed, and I dragged my burdened body in the direction of the drumming sound.

When I returned, there were butterflies with beautiful, colorful wings accompanying me home and honoring my return. Deep down, I knew that nature was communicating with me and celebrating my newfound identity and personal mission. Despite the intensity of this vision quest, I smiled from within and found the humor in it.

⠿

Remembering the moments of the initiatory journeys I had been through had given me a crystal-clear perspective of what

I was going through during the lockdown. It looked like what had happened during the vision quest with the Sequoioideae in 2015, my back-pain incident in Boulder in early 2019, and what I was experiencing through the current COVID-19 lockdown represented a single chain of events related to the very same injury.

However, that wasn't how it started. The earliest incident of a lower-back spine injury dated all the way back to early 2007, when I had an MRI scan that showed a hairline fracture on the L4 of my lumbar spine. It wasn't too long after that recovery that I decided to stop using medication, experienced topical steroid withdrawal, and embarked on a healing journey.

I realized that whether it was a vision quest with the Sequoioideae, my private conversation with the Universe in Encinitas, being immersed with ayahuasca in the Peruvian jungle, being in proximity of the white lions at Timbavati, meeting with the leopard shaman in Boulder, or being isolated here in a high-rise condominium in the boisterous city of Kuala Lumpur, they were all divine moments of *kairos*. They were created and beautifully designed by the Universe to awaken the entelechy within me. And they were all moments intentionally curated by the Divine Grace of the Universe.

The Universe is never absent during moments of darkness. It's the other way around! The Universe is more present than ever!

It was unfortunate that I had to experience the Universe through pain. But since it had already happened, I wasn't able to change the past. The only sensible option was to radically accept where I was at the moment. And such acceptance felt instantaneously liberating, because now I knew it had all been gifts from the Universe, just in strange wrapping paper.

The Universe had had my back all the while—I simply had not been aware of it. All of those journeys were optimal points to meet God halfway, and they were curated so that I would be able to open my divine eyes and see God in the world and in my divine heart to experience the Divine Grace of the Universe.

While I was learning from my past, I was also thinking about the smart thing to do in the present and future. It seemed like common sense to enjoy the ride of life while radically accepting the human pain and suffering that was right in front of me.

With this insight, I finally stopped trying to fix myself and surrendered my life into the hands of the Universe with absolute faith. I had done it way too many times in the past to know that at the end of the dark tunnel, there would always be a bright light from the Universe.

From that moment on, all thoughts of suicide completely vanished from my consciousness.

I guess Milarepa was right by putting his head into the demon's mouth!

CHAPTER SEVENTEEN

From Self-Righteousness to Self-Responsibility

Courage became an accidental trait that I developed. Time after time, when I was forced into situations of fear, and with radical acceptance of such human experience, courage was born. Yet during the critical moment of desiring to end my life, *accidental* courage transformed into *intentional* courage. It happened when I chose to accept the totality of the human experience each day.

As the days went by during the lockdown, nothing much changed on the outside. Things continued to be as chaotic as ever, if not worse. But there was something different about me. I started to appreciate the little things in life. I noticed that simple pleasures—like taking a shower, basking in the sun, or taking any opportunities I could to walk barefoot on the earth—created joyful moments in my life.

"The great awakening" had led me toward "the great softening" as I began to soften my heart in light of the difficult experiences I was having. I told myself that all I needed was the willingness to show up in the present moment. I didn't need to know *how*.

I lived each day as it *was* rather than what I expected it to be. I simply stopped trying so hard to figure out what was next. I took every opportunity to live fully in the moment rather than obsessing over my healing progress. It was with such a mindset and attitude that I was able to open my mind to the infinite possibilities, and open my heart to receive the Divine Grace of the Universe. Recognizing that I was a child of the Universe, I finally accepted that I deserved healing and needed help.

Every day, I made a commitment to myself to commune with the Universe by praying with reverence rather than begging for something. One day I was sitting in meditation, practicing my daily communion with the Universe. I was listening to the Heart Sutra, a popular religious text in Buddhism that is famous for the teaching "Form is emptiness, emptiness is form," which simply means that reality as it is may not be what we *think* it is.

Listening to the Heart Sutra, I was reminded of the leopard shaman, John Lockley, teaching me about the importance of emptying my spiritual cup. This led me into an insightful moment where I thought, *Perhaps all of my suffering is rooted in my own misperception of life, and as a consequence, my mind and body are maladapting with deep depression and chronic disease. If I am the creator of my deep depression and chronic disease, then I am the only one who can undo it!*

This insight opened me up to the Universe, and my prayers were spontaneously answered. This was a moment I called the *humbling*. I surrendered my ego and told the Universe, "I will do whatever you tell me to do. I humbly accept."

And without over-explaining anything, the Universe responded to me by presenting a single word: "Forgive!"

As soon as I heard that word, a form of light energy illuminated my consciousness from the top of my head and dived deep down into my bodily vessel, cleansing the mental impurities and bodily toxins within me. Tears poured out of my eyes. Right away, I got out of the lotus meditative position and fell onto my knees humbly as I wailed at the top of my lungs. It wasn't a cry of pain but one of profound love for life, its wonder, and its ordinary magic.

Ah, I remembered!

This wasn't the first time the Universe had presented me with a message of forgiveness. The very same message had been delivered to me when I was sitting in the plant-medicine ceremony with Grandmother Ayahuasca. It seemed that I had truly forgotten it, and now, I had been given an opportunity to *remember*—again! This time, remembrance pierced through the mental construct of my understanding of forgiveness and reached deep down into my bones, revealing its true meaning.

In the theatre of my mind, I saw myself holding on to the position of victimhood, where all I did was blame and prove others wrong. Yes, I was scarred from the past, when I had been innocent and vulnerable, but that didn't give me the right to persecute others.

I had not been able to let go of the fact that my parents, ancestors, doctors, teachers, spiritual mentors, and government—all of whom were supposed to protect the children—had failed me terribly. I was angry at the harm that had been perpetrated upon me because these individuals and entities had clung to their fixated beliefs rather than making the necessary changes to adapt to the situations at hand. I was frustrated that I had not been heard, seen, and acknowledged. I thought that everyone should have known better.

Hence, I wanted to prove all of them wrong.

I had persecuted them by punishing myself. I clung heavily to my identity as a victimized, sick child. I had kept myself in a state of disease with all that anger, and I was shown that only forgiveness was the remedy. Forgiveness showed me that it was the doorway for all forms of love to come through, and that included healing in the highest expression. Recognizing this truth, I was faced with a choice between self-righteousness and self-responsibility.

I asked the victimized part of me, *Would you rather be right, or would you rather be free and effective?*

Even if my victimhood was justified, self-righteousness would never have taken me to a place of healing. Self-righteousness had blinded me from seeing the possibilities and had perpetuated my misery. This was the spiritual lesson that was missing from my formal education. I had been arrogant with respect to my spiritual wisdom, and by learning this insight, I had to strip myself bare and step down from the pedestal of self-righteousness.

In that moment, I made a commitment to myself to accept this divine message by renouncing self-righteousness from my behavior, my thinking, and my life. I vowed to continue to soften my heart to express such love. I was now ready to lead a life filled with love and courage.

And in that moment, the truth set me free, and the *Homo luminous* within me bloomed into expression.

That same night, I asked my family to gather around me. With an open heart, I shared my struggles and the insights I had discovered. I asked for forgiveness from them and offered forgiveness for any harm done on both sides. The responses I received were mostly shock and confusion, but they did show up with love and attentiveness.

Verbal and intellectual understanding didn't have to occur between us. An authentic expression from the heart was enough. I had untethered a knot between us by simply expressing myself vulnerably. That opened up the greatest potential for healing, not just for me, but for them as well.

Through being tender, vulnerable, and open, we had released a type of possessive energy that kept us stuck, and through that release, all of us dropped into a sigh of relief. Finally, there was some space. For me, it was about tearing down the walls that had been protecting my vulnerable heart, freeing my inner demons rather than holding on to them, and subsequently, allowing my family into my heart. For them, they were finally able to be a part of my healing process by loving me unconditionally. They were witnesses to my truth, so healing was set in motion for all of us. I finally became comfortable in my own skin and was able to receive their love.

This was the moment when I was truly living up to my mythic name. Chiron didn't blame others for being wounded. Furthermore, he gave up his immortality and his godhood to release others from their prisons out of humility and compassion.

He didn't need to be righteous.

He didn't need to prove.

He didn't need to win.

Letting go of one's immortality and godhood was a symbolic language of surrendering one's own convictions of being right. As a result, truth emerged, and transcendental healing ensued.

Henceforth, I was initiated into my mythic name. I was truly living and embodying my mentor spirit. I was able to proudly call myself...*Chiron*.

Change was able to occur both in an instant and over a period of time. This held true for my healing as well. The moment when the truth set me free, I was able to open up to Divine Guidance and experience one meaningful event after another. It appeared that forgiveness wasn't just about letting go of the harm I had done to myself or what others had done to me, but also about liberating myself to trust my own choices and decisions. Forgiveness had led me to an openness of the heart and a spaciousness of the mind.

This was when I met Dr. Darren Weissman and was introduced to The LifeLine Technique®, an integrative system developed by Dr. Darren. He had taught many people how to befriend their subconscious mind in order to promote holistic healing. Through this technique, I was finally able to tie up all the loose knots of self-healing and self-actualization lessons from my past. Through our sessions together, I discovered that the limitations of my healing were confined to the comfort circle of my beliefs, which were embedded in my subconscious mind. The more I opened up to the possibility of healing, the more powerful the resilient healing force of nature came through.

As a result, healing occurred in the short span of three months, and I was in awe of this miracle.

How did it happen?

Why did it happen now but not before?

I learned that the subconscious mind had to be our collaborator instead of our enemy in order to bring forth healing, as well as our heart's greatest desire. Over the years of traveling in search for a remedy, I never once thought that this healing force existed within me all along. I had always believed that the remedy was somewhere *out there*. The tools, the techniques, the diet, the meditation, the lifestyle changes, and the habits and behavior hacks were all great, but they were incomplete without the right intention.

As part of the miracle of my healing, I was reminded that the greatest technology of all time was always nature. And the best part was that nature was all around me and within me. Nature was always accessible if I chose to connect with it. When my body was given the right conditions for healing, it simply thrived. I had learned that the right conditions weren't at all complicated or difficult. Instead, they were so simple that my conditioned mind had too much difficulty comprehending them.

I had successfully created trophic cascading within my body!

In the span of the next six months, healing continued to happen at all levels. Following the healing of my body, I found greater inner peace. Negative self-talk was still present, but it had no power over me anymore. When painful emotions arose, I was now able to be compassionate by showing up to myself with loving-kindness. My conversations and interactions with my family became more harmonious, even when we disagreed with each other. I was able to really feel comfortable in my own skin, and I started to form more authentic connections with people whom I enjoyed having deep and meaningful conversations with.

Following my healing, I started to share my knowledge with those who were struggling during the lockdown. I reached out to people and gave free sessions to help them learn how to align their subconscious minds in conjunction with The LifeLine Technique. My research continued, and every day I was awed by the results I was receiving. I was convinced that if I wasn't the only one experiencing miraculous healing, then whatever this miracle was had a science and a system that followed nature's law of love and respect.

Wonder and ordinary magic became part of my daily life again. I now embodied both the creative innocence of a child and the maturity of a wise adult. In moments of trials and tribulations—whether it was mine or others'—I was now able to show up powerfully to lead and guide anyone on my path toward their own greater evolution. And although I worked hard, I was still able to maintain my connection to wonder and ordinary magic, and I asked for guidance from the Universe anytime I felt lost.

In a short period of time, I had learned that creating healing conditions in the human system was all about creating connectedness. And what connected everything and anything was *love*. During The LifeLine Technique sessions, I was finally able to understand that when the heart, which is the sovereign leader of our human system, steps up and rises to leadership by making authentic and truthful choices in life, the rest of the healing process is history.

Love connects; fear separates.

Our conscious and subconscious minds have to communicate with each other. People need to talk with one another and resolve their conflicts with love. Systems of nature have to communicate with each other so that symbiosis can occur. And the cell-signaling system of our body needs to be linked for homeostasis to happen. Also, energy needs to flow within the living system in order for healing to occur. *Love creates flow, whereas fear creates stagnancy.*

I had learned that disease, premature aging, and early deaths were initiatory signs from the Universe so that we can learn the greater lessons of life. These signs do not apply only to individuals but are reflected in the greater dysfunctions of the collective as well.

I once heard a perspective that originated from a wise Native American who confirmed my observation: when diseases manifested in an individual, they reflected the disconnection of the community as a whole from the harmony of nature. Instead of shunning or isolating the diseased individuals, as we often did in the city, the entire community came together to offer gratitude, blessings, and love to them. Instead of blaming the diseased ones for creating discord in the community, people learned to understand the changes that needed to happen on a social and communal level. A disease was never seen as an isolated biological pathology, but a reflection of the problems that were surfacing in the collective environment. When all those issues were resolved, the symptoms of the disease vanished accordingly, and greater harmony within the community was experienced and celebrated.

The symptoms of disease, premature aging, and premature death were never the problems to be solved in the first place. They were sacred messengers that held important information about the conditions of our society, our environment, and our spirituality—how well we were participating in the circle of life.

As humans, we're never just biological beings, so we require more than biological interventions to promote our health. We are social beings who need a sense of belonging and meaningful connection to survive and thrive. We are also mental and emotional beings who are capable of self-awareness, creating meaning, discovering our purpose, and bringing our creations to life. In addition, we are spiritual beings who are connected to the unknown forces of this mysterious universe, and we seek out the evolution of our individual consciousness. Ultimately, we are all energetic beings who are, on a fundamental level, pure energy that is vibrating down at the atomic level.

As I began to know myself on such a grand scale, I saw that health wasn't about the absence of symptoms but more about the presence of deep connection and communication between the social, mental, emotional, spiritual, and energetic parts of me. This deep connection allowed homeostasis to function at its best.

With homeostasis, anything that is out of balance is able to return to balance. Homeostasis helped me return to balance and quiescence, which I experienced as love, peace, and harmony. And each time I returned to balance, I became more immune to stress, crises, and adversities, while evolving my consciousness and maturing closer to my entelechy. When I learned to read the true messages of my symptoms or those of others, I was able to continually bring myself or anyone else back to homeostasis—not just on a biological level, but also on a social, mental, emotional, spiritual, and energetic level.

I believe that our personal healing is never simply self-serving, but actually has the ability to serve and contribute to the collective, especially to all of life in nature. Healed people have the capacity to heal others simply because they emanate and embody love, light, and truth, which are reflections of fundamental natural and universal laws. Love is the invisible force that governs all and heals all. When a disease, crisis, or conflict is observed from that position of loving awareness, innate wisdom and intelligence naturally follow through to resolve the issue. This is indeed the very same wonder and ordinary magic I knew as a child and had forgotten as an adult.

In fact, this was the missing link that all of our modern healers and medical practitioners seemed to have forgotten. They had forgotten that nature was the source of healing, not them. The best any healer can do is facilitate healing and create conducive conditions so that the nature within can do what it's able to do best.

Strangely, it wasn't until I had exhausted all possible approaches from my search for healing abroad that I finally turned within and discovered another way. The journeys that I had taken had not been futile and pointless, though, because I finally understood what John Lockley had been pointing me toward—to empty my spiritual cup and reconnect with my roots. Without having experienced these crises, I never would have directly experienced what it meant to go through the dark tunnel of the human experience.

Now that I had arrived at the other end of that tunnel, I was able to understand why my life had turned out the way that it had. All the years of trial and error had finally culminated into the discovery of this missing link of healing. I saw my past pain as a blessing in disguise, giving me this opportunity to know myself, love myself, and heal myself through the mysterious invisible force of wonder and ordinary magic.

I was finally able to become *Homo luminous*.

EPILOGUE

Calling: The Courage to Be Ordinarily Me

"What is impossible from the eyes of yesterday is possible from the eyes of tomorrow. And the present moment is the doorway to infinite possibilities."

—Chiron Yeng

I was ready.
Ideas, memorized.
Words, recited.
Mindset, focused.
Energy, centered.

My life flashed before me. Memories of the past—both the breakdowns and the breakthroughs—rushed forward. They all came together as if woven from golden threads made out of wonder and ordinary magic, showing me how deeply I had lived in the tapestry of my life.

My nervous system was aroused, and my awareness was heightened. I felt the rapture of being alive, and I was reminded of my days sitting in ceremony with the plant-medicine ayahuasca. My senses were so aroused that I couldn't tell if I was excited or fearful.

As I was standing backstage at a TEDx event where I would be speaking, I wondered how many moments like this I would be able to experience in my lifetime. There were some who contemplated that such moments only occurred when one was about to face death. But over the years of my life, moments of death had happened so many times that I felt like I was starting to get used to it. Again, I was grateful that deathlike experiences had found me while I was still alive.

I felt great. I was excited and hopeful and also very present and focused, calm and confident, and I was more than ready to give the speech of my life.

Destiny was right in front of me.

After months of curating my stories and after hours of rehearsal, the red circle on the main stage was finally within my sight. It was only a matter of moments before I stepped into that red circle to present my story in front of 1,500 seated audience members (and 150 volunteers who'd helped me put this event together).

It was a rite of passage.

I knew that sharing my story on this platform would be the catalyst to change me forever. In the eyes of others, it might have looked like I was an authority sorts and was receiving recognition and respect. But for me, I saw this as the culmination of an important chapter of my life. It was the doorway to the liberation of my suffering and the evolution of stepping into a new life altogether.

Completing my healing process meant the world to me. It was my moment to experience a mythological transformation from suffering into a form of enlightenment, just like the Greek god Chiron had transformed into a constellation in the sky. My diseases and neuroses were about to be reborn into a new form of higher aspirations. This meant that the emotional weight of my suffering was about to be given away as a contribution to the circle of life. I would finally be able to lift it off of my tiresome shoulders and my burdened heart. I could present my personal journey as a symbolic and meaningful message that could guide other individuals' healing journeys.

Stories like this in human history have given people hope and wonder. Within those accounts, there was a glimpse of possibility that no matter how intense the pain we were going through, it was possible for us to heal and transcend too.

I once shared my story with a good friend whose years were beyond mine. He was close in age to my father, yet there was no intergenerational separateness in our conversations. We were able to communicate as equals, mutual kindred spirits who were both on journeys of healing and trying to excavate the meaning of human suffering through our own experiences.

He was a knowledgeable and courageous man whose story was so powerful that he reflected the resilience of the human spirit, which enabled him to understand the enigmatic nature of the Divine Grace of the Universe.

We both agreed that love was the missing ingredient when it came to healing anything at all. Whether it was a physical illness, a mental neurosis, an emotional turmoil, or a spiritual crisis, love was the solution. He shared that when stories of transformation were told—especially when they were tales of insurmountable suffering that transformed into the expression of the highest human potential—the powerful emotion of gratitude was invoked within others. In return, this gratitude created a cascade of neurochemistry within the body that was responsible for healing on a cellular level.

How powerful!

When I heard my friend's story and reflected upon my own, I truly found a deeper experience of gratitude with respect to my life and my healing journey. His story wasn't mine to tell, but in this meaningful connection, I was certain that the human spirit was resilient by nature, and there were many more individuals out there who had stories as powerful as ours.

Now here I was on October 22, 2022, D-Day for speakers to present their most heartfelt stories and brilliant ideas. I felt the same visceral and bodily sensation of gratitude when I had shared stories with my friend. The only difference was that this was amplified exponentially.

Only those who were present in person for TEDxPetaling Street 2022 knew the power of the heart-opening experience of that day. Through the law of resonance, and through the speakers' stories, the energy of gratitude was passed on to others through the invisible field, creating a wave of healing through the collective.

And to my honor, I wasn't the only one who stood upon that stage. Along with me were fellow Malaysians who shared the same unwavering courage to follow our hearts' passions. Similar to me, they were individuals who had walked through hardships in their lives, all for the sake of fulfilling a certain divine purpose that they had intrinsically felt. Their human spirits had guided them step by step along their journeys, and ultimately, allowed us to converge, meet, and speak in the middle of that stage.

Perhaps it was the very same wonder and ordinary magic that had brought them here. All of us were travelers in our own lives, individuals who had accepted the call to adventure—who were walking the road less traveled. The silent camaraderie between all of us was exciting, as it reminded me of the sense of belonging and collective interconnectedness we all shared. Despite being strangers, there was a knowing that we were being woven together by the Divine Grace of the Universe to create a grand tapestry of human-consciousness evolution. While waiting to get onstage, I whispered to myself, "Wow! How did each of us come together in this way? What was the invisible force of the Universe that brought us here?"

Countless inspirational thinkers, creatives, and innovators had stood on that red circle before me. On that day, though, TEDxPetalingStreet was more than just people sharing lofty ideas—there were also stories worth honoring. The speakers who shared the stage with me on that day had their own personal journeys to walk through and unique callings from the Universe to accept. That red circle had transformed lives of millions of people throughout the world, and it was finally our turn to stand on it.

Just like Olympians carrying a torch, which symbolizes the passing down of the flame of spirit, knowledge, and life, TEDx events have something similar. Instead of athletes, TEDx has speakers who are all in their own right keepers of humanity's new ideas, inspiring knowledge, and timeless wisdom. They stand on that red circle with the intention of illuminating human ignorance and elevating human consciousness.

Instead of the Olympic flame, we were passing on the fire of Prometheus, which symbolizes the advancement of humans' inner and outer technology.

Taking the mantle of those before me, I felt like a cog in a wheel of the Universe's wonder to share the spirit of human resilience and the power of healing through love. Everyone was waiting to hear and remember such a miracle. I felt as if the collective was calling out to me to open others' hearts and minds—and most important of all, to remember the possibility of living the beautiful human life we all knew was possible.

Being invited to be part of this event was surreal. The impostor syndrome within me was asking, *Who are you to be standing next to these amazing people?* Even so, these negative thoughts were of little concern to me because I knew I had something powerful and moving to share.

Eighteen months prior to stepping on this stage, after my symptoms miraculously subsided at the end of 2020, I knew that the healing process had to continue. I was aware that if I was to completely heal, I needed to understand health at a fundamental level. The etymology of the word *health* is *hale*, derived from the Old English language of Germanic origin and meaning "to be whole, a thing that is complete in itself."

As such, I started my solopreneur journey as a spiritual health practitioner to help others reach their greatest human potential. My role was to help people—especially highly sensitive individuals like me—lead with the subconscious mind, rather than being driven by it. I saw that when the subconscious mind is aligned with the conscious mind through loving awareness of the heart, the deepest desires of the soul are revealed. As such, it's a no-brainer for people to go after what they want, and that was when I witnessed miracles in them. I saw that all forms of pain were transformed into greater purpose and, subsequently, the desired physical healing follows.

A fulfilled soul is an individual who is purpose driven. In their fulfillment, they are experiencing wholeness. And within the experience of wholeness, the body produces a cascade of neurochemistry and biochemistry that inspires physical regeneration. The beauty of the mind-body connection is revealed in the behavior of those individuals. They become serious about their healing journeys, curious about the possibilities of life, and come to appreciate simple pleasures and fully commit to actualizing their entelechy. Their eyes glow, and they have the courage to tread the unknown.

The common thread between all of us is that we have an honest yearning to find our calling, to reconnect with our divine purpose, to remember wonder and ordinary magic, and to finally come home to the Divine Grace of the Universe, and ultimately ourselves. Naturally, after the completion of such a journey, many of us want to contribute our gifts and skills to those who need them most.

I saw that there is a universal path within us highly sensitive souls even though we were walking in our very own unique directions. I recognized that this universal path begins with being aware of what is wrong with us; having the self-compassion to unlearn, relearn, and transform those limitations; overcome trials and tribulations to evolve into new selves; and finally, dedicate the unique wisdom that we have harvested from our lives to serve the growth of others.

Perhaps the Universe had created highly sensitive individuals in the world to rise into heart-centered leaders who could serve the planetary consciousness evolution and healing. We were made to show others that sensitivity was part of being absolutely and ordinarily human. Rather than a flaw, a weakness, or a curse, maybe our human sensitivity has been our greatest strength all along. I believed that rising into a heart-centered leader who led and healed with love was exactly the new paradigm of being that was going to make the old, limiting models of both leadership and healing obsolete.

Ah! I finally found what I was looking for ever since my query in Timbavati.

Indeed—to love is to lead, and to lead is to love!
Similarly—to love is to heal, and to heal is to love!

As I stepped into this work, I realized that it was a different ball game now. When I was sick and out of action, I had my own problems to deal with, and that was it. That was the easy part. Being a spiritual health practitioner who facilitates spiritual transformation within others, I had to be responsible for others who desired to move through difficult emotions and painful human experiences. And on top of that, I had to go through my own at the same time.

The only way I was able to keep myself accountable to such an important and honorable process was to continue to deepen my healing and self-actualization process. What mattered most wasn't my skills or my wisdom, but the presence I was embodying when I showed up to hold a sacred transformational space for others. Yet, through these experiences, I found that in healing others, I was also healing myself. Similarly, by healing myself, I was also healing others. I became a noble guide to help people move through times of darkness when they weren't able to do so for themselves.

In comparison to how I had functioned in the past, I now intentionally sought healing instead of waiting to be healed. I didn't need to wait for the Divine Grace of the Universe to show up. Healing was work that was never done. We never just healed from our symptoms and that was it: We won! Yay! Instead, healing was a lifelong dedication to becoming whole and being in right relationship with this earth. Otherwise, the symptoms of disease would return. Our physical health was never the cause, but an outgrowth of the larger dysfunctional environment that we lived in. Hence, I believed that I was only truly able to be healed when all others were healed, since we were all interconnected.

By transforming myself, I transform the world. It starts with me.

My solopreneur journey had led me to many heart-opening synchronicities. While working on myself, one of my tasks was to have a clear vision of what success meant to me. I remembered writing down the many forms of success clearly— having financial freedom, cultivating harmonious interactions with my family members, attaining perfect health with an athletic body, meeting the love of my life, creating impactful business collaborations, and being on the TEDx platform to share my transformational healing story—and they all came true.

I had definitely courageously loved myself into a life of wonder and ordinary magic. And all it took—was to be ordinarily me.

What a miracle life is!

⸬

And there I was, feeling all of the energy in the hall while recalling the memories of the past. Wonder and ordinary magic was definitely flooding through the room. I was standing backstage waiting for my turn to receive the limelight while waiting for the UITM Chamber Choir to complete their chorus. Befittingly, the title of their song was "Sing Till Our Hearts Echo."

There was something divine about their orchestrated performance. The harmony and the resonance of their vocals wasn't just pleasant to the ears, but also penetrated into the hearts of the collective, including mine. It shook my soul awake, snapping me out of my mind's neurosis, forcing tears to run down my cheeks uncontrollably.

In that short moment, I thought a lot about my name, Chiron, and how it symbolically resembled my birth name 益庭 (yì tíng), which was given to me by my parents. Since I had been young, and throughout the decade when I had traveled around the world to search for my authentic self, I had resented my birth name without understanding why. But little did I know that I was playing out a life that was encrypted symbolically in my given name.

An enlightening insight struck me, and in an instant, I realized the deeper meaning of my own birth name. I saw that the word 益 (yì) was able to be translated as "ever-growing and constantly evolving," and the word 庭 (tíng) was able to be translated as "a courtyard, family, or a home." When I put them together, my name was all about creating an ever-growing and constantly evolving home.

I had set out into the world to look for myself, only to come home to my country to realize that I was the one I was looking for. The ever-growing and constantly evolving home was never a place in the world, but a spiritual home that was within my ordinary self. Similar to Chiron's myth, it wasn't about healing his wounds of abandonment, rejection, and betrayal or sacrificing his immortality, but to go home to where he belonged, in the sky, as a constellation.

With that realization, I had a profound appreciation for my birth name and recalled the different thread of stories about the sacrifices made by my ancestors to lead me here. With that, I knew that my parents who named me were proud of me, just as I was proud of myself. It was a full circle from birth all the way to this moment, only to be reborn and owning the essence of my birth name. This time, it was all from my own efforts and by my own choice.

I'm coming home.

Before I knew it, all of my preparation to go onstage was shattered, and I got lost in the euphoric state of love for being alive, along with a deep appreciation for my newfound realization of my ordinary self. But although I had heard that the fear of public speaking was more intense than the fear of death, I wasn't afraid at all. It was the complete opposite—I was ecstatic. It was funny to experience the same type of arousal of the nervous system that, when given a different context, gave rise to a completely different experience.

While people were receiving calm impressions from me, I was actually topsy-turvy from within, ready to crash into the couch and pass out. My legs were wobbly, and I didn't know if my voice was going to sound okay. My carefully memorized thoughts, recited words, focused mindset, and centered energy were all for naught, and I felt the calling from spirit to free myself and to allow my truth to let itself loose. There was no holding back anymore.

Time expanded when I stepped onto the stage. It felt like an eternity that I immersed myself in the attention of more than a thousand pairs of eyes. The stage felt so big, and I felt so small and insignificant. I wasn't able to see individual faces in the audience, so it was as if I was giving a talk to myself. It was between me and me. I took a pause, deeply breathing into my soul, and at some point, spirit took over me. Before I knew it, the entire speech had gone by in a flash.

I have very little memory of what happened onstage. I don't

remember how I did or if I did enough to share the treasure trove of wisdom that lived within me. I was tempted to analyze my performance, but it was what it was. Bigger forces were at play, and I was simply relieved that it was all over. I thought I was giving the world something, yet it felt like the opposite— I was receiving something very precious from the audience.

Tears were shed by those from diverse walks of life. Whether we were the organizers and the volunteers, the speakers, the sponsors, or the audience, we had something to take away and something to give. We were all inspiring one another. And it was one of those rare moments when I found the power of collective efforts creating something larger than our own egos. It was also a rare moment for me to feel welcomed, and I experienced a unique sense of belonging to the Malaysian community after being in foreign countries for so many years.

Yes, I'm finally home.

Eighteen minutes onstage felt like years, and maybe, lifetimes. Stepping out there felt like I had entered another dimension. The stage felt like a wormhole into a different portal. Everything was the same, but felt different. The air felt lighter, and my body charged with energy that I didn't know was possible. Even sex didn't feel like this. I had been a performer all my life and had stepped onto big stages through the performing arts. Yet there was nothing like this.

The person who stepped onto the stage and the person who stepped down from it were two completely different people. It was a rite of passage marking the death of the victimized sick child, and the birth of the peaceful warrior who embodied profound wisdom because he'd shared it with the world and was a witness to his truth.

I turned from a boy into a man who knew himself, loved himself, remembered his wonder and ordinary magic, had healed through the Divine Grace of the Universe, and finally come home to his authentic expression of *Homo luminous*.

Afterword

"God has entrusted me with myself. No man is free who is not master of himself. A man should so live that his happiness shall depend as little as possible on external things. The world turns aside to let any man pass who knows where he is going."

—Epictetus

Life is precious. It is fleeting yet pervasive. No one can hold on to it. The greatest beauty of life is its impermanence. We yearn to relive our bliss and re-create the memories that give us the greatest joy. Nevertheless, such intention and emotional grasping is exactly what is tampering with what has given us the bliss in the first place.

Life is unforgiving that way. One choice and we're all down the road of no return. Our concern isn't really whether we make right or wrong choices but whether we're truly living our choices fully. There are no good or bad choices, just those that keep us the same, and those that change our lives forever.

We are all whole to begin with. We never lack anything, nor are we too much of anything. Our life journey isn't about addition or subtraction, but is simply a growing expression of who we already are. We are nature's masterpiece of unfolding from within into an outward expression. Our outward beauty is our spirit expressing its essence.

Imagine that you're a blank piece of paper that is folding and unfolding itself into the next greatest origami sculpture. Whatever shape you take the form of, you're still that paper. You don't know what the end product looks like, but you at least know the next best step. Perhaps taking the next step from one moment to another is enough.

The life that is throbbing within us cannot be measured. It is unconditional, and nothing that we chase on the outside can truly match what is within us. We tend to describe a throbbing feeling as bliss, and it has a peculiar motivation to guide our actions through our human desires. Feeling this bliss is good enough for us to follow its lead because it is our very spirit that is guiding us toward our entelechy. This throbbing feeling is an energetic sensation in the body; it isn't just a mere concept. It's deeply experiential, ecstatic, and euphoric, and happening in the here and now. This experience cannot be rationalized by scientific means and isn't to be idealized as a spiritual heaven that is far away in our deluded imagination.

Our perception fools us—all the time. What we see is not the entirety of reality as it is. We neither see ultraviolet light nor infrared spectrums but that doesn't mean they are not present and can't be felt or experienced. Similarly, the feeling of life throbbing within us can't be seen, but perhaps we can learn to experience it and feel it in and through our bodies. Bliss is present all of the time, accessible, and trainable to our senses. It is our natural state of being when we're completely ordinary, immersed in the present moment, which is in the deep now. Inquisitive spiritual practitioners call it the mind-body connection, heart-brain coherence, or integration of the spirit into our bodies. I prefer to call it *wonder and ordinary magic.*

We can choose to spend our lives chasing our own tails and obsessing over insignificant matters. Or we can choose to come into peace, joy, and harmony at every given moment to feel the rapture of being alive.

Living and being is simpler than we think.

All it takes is for all of us to be willing—the willingness to be here, right now, radically accepting all of life that is happening in this present moment. Yet, the simple path is not an easy one. It is a path that renounces comfort, certainty, and conformity. The simple path is to express the potential of the moment, which is completely ordinary yet powerfully mesmerizing. It is the shortest and longest path we will ever take.

What is already here has no form, but there is an essence, an experience, a desire, that longs to take form. As such, the mystery of the Universe is seeking to be known, through and as us. We are the creative expression of the Divine Grace of the Universe, and that is to be revered with honor and gratitude.

If the mystery of the Universe is the question, then its subjects are the answer.

If the Universe calls, we answer.

So, the question you may be confronted with is this: *How far are you willing to go to know that life is precious, to re-*

member your wonder and ordinary magic, to experience the Universe as a true mirror of the love within you, and to actualize your entelechy in the service of life?

Choosing this path is never about being free from pain, fear, and stress. It is never about freedom from disease, broken relationships, scarcity, or chaos—or the freedom *from* anything at all. Instead, it is the freedom *to* our entelechy, which is all about the evolution of our consciousness. Our true freedom is about radically accepting all of these aspects of our human experience in order to know our ever-expanding and ever-evolving expression of *Homo luminous*.

This is the path of the peaceful warrior.

It is the path of knowing the truth of who we are, courageously loving our ordinariness, and committing to healing ourselves by becoming whole again. And if you know that this is the path you choose, then there are only two mistakes you can make: not starting upon it, and not seeing things through to the end in order to experience the truth of the matter.

The cosmic joke about this path is that the work is never done, just like the evolution and revolution of the circle of life never stops. Healing and self-actualization are both never finished, never completed. Change is the only constant of the Universe.

We're always chasing after the horizon—yet, ignorantly, we're blind to see that the horizon expands infinitely and we're never going to arrive to savor it. We often make false promises to ourselves that we will finally feel fulfilled, complete, and ultimately free when we reach a certain outcome. Hence, like running on a hamster wheel, we chase after the delusional carrot that we're never going to reach. It is never enough for the human mind. Our happiness and freedom end up becoming highly conditional, and that turns us into hungry ghosts who can never be satiated.

I often wonder if our human lives are simply reduced to this existential rat race. I find that the perpetual chase doesn't just limit the capitalistic chase for material wealth and financial freedom; it also involves noble causes such as creating environmental well-being, achieving social equality, healing global crises, eradicating the rise of diseases in the world, empowering personal growth, and developing conscious communities with spiritual values.

It doesn't matter which game we choose to play. The outcome is always the same.

If we're honest enough with ourselves, it's always about fulfilling an inner lack that is a bottomless black hole. Every time we achieve something, there are many more problems that arise. We're never at peace and truly living in the moment. It is like we're made and conditioned to chase.

It is easy to assume that we're broken, but actually what is broken isn't our beinghood or the world, but our very own worldviews. It is tempting to sympathize with our own conditions, but what we need isn't more advice or solutions but to be believed in, especially for our unique path of individuation.

We need support from others to be seen for the sovereignty of our true nature because when we're in our darkness, we can't see the reflection of our true nature.

We need mentors and comrades who have walked such a path so that we understand that what we're going through is an opportunity for a more awakened and resilient reality.

We need to know that at the end of the dark tunnel is a brilliant light, and behind the futility of chasing after a horizon that we're never going to reach, there is a beautiful human experience waiting for us, and the Divine Grace of the Universe is present in the making of who we are.

What needed to die isn't our beinghood, but our egocentric attachments to chasing after an outcome. The nihilism and all the suicide ideations represent the desire to kill our own egos. The emptiness that we feel isn't any form of scarcity or lack, but the presence of space that is so full of potential waiting to be birthed. Hence, what needed to be transformed was our false perception of separateness.

The cosmic joke is now a cosmic misunderstanding.

With the death of separateness comes the birth of connectedness. We are never participants chasing after the horizon. We are the horizon expanding our comfort zones. As we expand, we experience greater diversity from this Universe and experience more possible expressions of our unique creativity.

In our connectedness, we know that we are already whole and complete to begin with. And within that wholeness, we have the opportunity to express many different shapes and forms of our potential. Life, then, isn't about chasing to become or to attain something, but to live in the moment as creators of our very own desires. Our day-to-day approach is to create more wonder and ordinary magic, where the finite game of win or lose becomes an infinite game of creativity and innovation.

This is the beginning of the beautiful life we know is possible.

A beautiful life is not one without pain, fear, and stress, but rather, it is one in which our capacity is to be at peace and in harmony with those difficult human experiences. Those experiences continuously show us where we're blind, and they are catalysts to our human transformation. We are in the perpetual process of awakening to the greater divinity of who we are, expanding our consciousness to be interconnected with all while upholding our unique expression of *Homo luminous*.

Spiritual callings, as you have experienced with me all throughout this book, do not appear out of nowhere. They begin with faint and gentle whispers. Most of the time they were letting me know about the disconnection of my conditioned reality, which was in no way ordinary, natural, or healthy. Through my diseased state, the Universe showed me that we humans were completely separated from nature, and the constructs of governance were egocentric and unsustainable. As such, everything that we had been doing from the micro level to the macro level only perpetuated more separation and destruction.

The calling to be a peaceful warrior has very little to do with solving these problems, but is instead an invitation to reconnect to our true nature. It is all about remembering that we're whole to begin with, and that we have an invitation to return to the wonder and ordinary magic of life. It is all about remembering deep connection and love through the Divine Grace of the Universe, which is usually present amid our pain and suffering.

Healing requires us to drop our defenses, to be humble enough to listen attentively, and to be vulnerable enough to feel the hurt of our humanity. Just like crustaceans need to shed their initial shells to grow, and caterpillars need to dissolve themselves in cocoons to become butterflies, humans need to disintegrate their egos in order to transform into loving and conscious humans.

Only then can the Divine Grace of the Universe act upon us, in and through us, and as us. The struggle to embark on such a path is that there is no written formula; hence, we have to constantly confront uncertainty. More drastically, the deeper struggle is to divert completely from the ways, mindset, and behaviors of what is considered normal.

This is why I resisted the call for many years. But eventually, the call became too loud for me to ignore, and I was forced to walk on the path of the peaceful warrior. I learned that it was futile to resist the call of the Universe. Most of the time I felt helpless, and wondered why this "special" treatment had only befallen me. I thought that life was going against me and that I was being punished to repay karmic debts.

Instead, the truth of the matter is that the Universe loves me so much that it wants to show me my true desire and help me realize my highest potential. Another truth is that I'm not the only one. There are many who are called and who are being initiated.

This story is unique to me, but the path is universal to us all.

⬚⬚

Writing this book was a journey of its own, and it took courage and faith to complete it. As such, this book went through several iterations where it had to be rewritten multiple times because it didn't look like an offering of wisdom to the world. Instead, it started off as a journal in which I was lamenting my victimized life; basically, it was a philosophical discourse about suffering. This was a sign of the disconnection between my heart, my mind, and my body. Thus, the writing journey of this book became a journey from the head to the heart, and finally into an embodiment of who I am. Through countless cycles of processing my inner wounds and purifying my psyche, I was able to tap into the deeper wisdom that was seeking to be expressed through my life's journey. I started to embody a newfound presence of unconditional love and acceptance for myself and the world that I thought was not possible before.

I owe my newfound wisdom to The LifeLine Technique, which helped me understand my subconscious mind and gave me tangible tools to bridge the gap between my wounds and my highest potential. The purification and transformational process led to a deeper connection between my heart, my mind, and my body, which helped me convey the deeper aspirations I wanted to share with the world.

This was when I realized that this book was something that I wanted to leave behind for future generations so they could remember who I was and understand the knowledge I had gained from this great mystery of life. In that respect, I found great joy in writing, as the experience showed me the wonder and ordinary magic that lived within my pain. The completion of this work gave me peace of mind, and I felt as if I had completed a pertinent chapter in my life's work.

So in closing, my final aspiration for you, my readers, is that you seek not from the outside but from within. Begin your own life quest. Turn inward and start writing about your own resilient human journey. Initiate your journey from the head to the heart, excavate wisdom from your life, and turn this knowledge into an embodiment of who you are.

Know yourself, and write down your very own personal philosophy. Then, love yourself! Love yourself deeply, make space for your hurt, and allow its deeper purpose to be revealed to you. Only then will you reemerge and become the authentic expression of *Homo luminous*.

You don't need to have great ambitions like getting your work published or becoming a best-selling author—that isn't the point. Instead, simply write in order to discover the true essence of your humanity. It is within your very life that the Universe has encoded secret messages leading to your true freedom and actualizing your greatest healing potential.

Be like Mahatma Gandhi who, when asked in an interview to give a message to the people, said, "Why should I send a message? My life is my message!"

Your life is indeed your message.

More than words, you are the living book that is walking on the face of this earth.

More than expectations, have the courage to love yourself and be ordinarily *you*.

That is when you become extraordinary.

Acknowledgements
(with Infinite Love and Gratitude)

No type of success is achieved alone. We often underestimate how much help we need from others to make our wishes come true.

This book is more than just my own creation; it is the result of the contributions of the many who have crossed my path. They have offered me timeless wisdom, loving energy exchanges, and life experiences that cannot be found through any form of education. As Paulo Coelho famously shared in his book *The Alchemist*, there is an ineffable force in the universe that conspires to help us achieve our desires. This statement is incredibly accurate in describing the creation of anything—whether it be a book, a business, a living being, or an ecosystem. Everything is entangled, and all beings collaborate to bring forth each other's creation.

The Universe is powerful beyond our comprehension, and the most miraculous thing is that this ineffable intelligence resides within each and every one of us. We're all interconnected, designed to help each other bring forth our deepest desires and our greatest creative potential.

To begin, I wish to express gratitude to my teachers and mentors:

I am grateful to *Dr. Darren Weissman* for bravely walking his path and becoming the epitome of what it means to be a mentor and leader who leads with love. I appreciate all the effort he put into creating The LifeLine Technique, teaching it to me, and sharing the power of infinite love and gratitude that facilitated my healing and transformation.

I express my gratitude to *Maurice Fernandez* for teaching me the coded language of astrology and helping me navigate moments of darkness and confusion. I thank him for guiding me to make sense of my life experiences and for his contribution of knowledge in understanding the development and evolution of human consciousness. I am grateful for his efforts in passing on wisdom from astrological ancestors to me, and for initiating me into the path of becoming a soul-centered astrologer.

I am grateful to *Roman Hanis and the Paititi Institute* for compassionately holding space for me during an ayahuasca ceremony and providing a safe environment for me to explore the depths of my soul and the vastness of my consciousness. I thank Roman for his leadership, and the support of the Paititi community for accelerating my healing and transformational journey, reconnecting me to Mother Nature in the Andes Mountains, and helping me remember my human essence.

I extend my gratitude to *Linda Tucker, Mae Naude, Wynter Worsthorne, Brad Laughlin, and the Global White Lions Protection Trust* for welcoming me to the lands of the white lions, teaching me the laws of lionhearted leadership, and inspiring me to reclaim my sovereign nature by courageously celebrating this world despite its darkness. I thank the white lions for reflecting the intelligence of nature that exists within me.

I give thanks to *Michael Jospé and the facilitators of the Earth-Based Institute* for teaching me the ancient wisdom of tracking and providing the foundational knowledge for me to become a transformational life coach today. I am so grateful for this training, which continues to open up my sensitivity and my connection to my gut instincts and intuition, which have become my greatest assets in my coaching work.

I am grateful to the professors, teachers, practitioners, staff members, and friends of *Naropa University*, especially *Ramon Parish and Jeanine Canty*, who provided a conducive educational environment for me to experiment with and research my spiritual journey.

I am also thankful to *Fain Tsai*, who lovingly shared her wisdom of Buddhism with me and enlightened my understanding of the energetic and unseen phenomena of the universe.

I express gratitude to *Hira Hosen*, who walked her path of ascension with utmost dedication. I am honored to receive her "Awakening the Illuminated Heart" teachings and to be initiated into the activation of the Mer-Ka-Ba. I am thankful for the loving space of deep healing and connection to universal love that she provided, and for her contribution to my spiritual ascension and the healing of my earthly body.

Last, I want to honor *Dr. Kulvi Kaur* for bridging the gap between science and spirituality and showing the parallel correlation between epigenetics and mysticism. I am grateful for her for showcasing that our human body is truly a wonder of the Universe.

Some teachers don't come in human form. Life is a place where we make mistakes and learn transformational lessons. This is why it is often called the *Earth School*. We all come here with imperfections and limitations, and our life stressors provide feedback on where we can make changes to align with the laws of nature. Despite how random life may seem, there are governing forces at work. Along my journey, I've discovered and become acquainted with the principles of synchronicity, which are sometimes referred to as meaningful coincidences. This is the feeling of being in the right place at the right time, doing the right thing. Nevertheless, synchronicity doesn't always feel good all the time. Synchronicity can also happen when it feels wrong, painful, and stressful.

I thank these teachers who showed up in other forms:

I am grateful to the animal kingdom and the animal spirits, as well as the plant kingdom and the plant spirits, who have communicated with me and blessed me with their wisdom of nature.

I give thanks to the invisible and elemental forces of nature, both light and dark, for guiding me to see the true nature of life.

I am also grateful to the ancestors, masters, and practitioners who were torchbearers of human enlightenment and dedicated their lives to contribute timeless wisdom to humanity. It's because of them that I've had the opportunity to be awakened spiritually.

Finally, I give thanks to all of my mistakes, blind spots, negative thinking, self-destructive habits, and self-sabotaging behaviors. They have shown me my imperfections and limitations, which I continually learn to transform as I actualize my true nature.

For many years, I searched for answers beyond borders and walked on different continents around the world. Little did I know that the answers I sought were right in my own backyard. When we look too far and wide, we become myopic and fail to appreciate the importance of the people and beings closest to us. I learned this the hard way: life isn't about seeking answers, but about living fully in the presence of those closest to us, so that truths are revealed to us. Coming full circle, I now recognize the necessity of acknowledging the love, support, and life lessons of those closest to us.

I am grateful to my family, my parents, and my lineage, who provided me with the resources and opportunities to embark on this journey of remembrance.

I am also grateful to my friends and allies—particularly *Vancelee Teng, Albert Lou, and Norman Chella,* who discussed spirituality and metaphysics, and shared creative expressions with me, helping me develop my own ideas about who I am and what I'm here to do.

I express gratitude to my lovers of the past, present, and future, who showed me intimacy and how to evolve into a fearless lover. They taught me what it means to be a man in this world.

I thank those with whom I have had conflicts, as they have helped me see where I was blinded and where boundaries weren't respected. I humbly apologize for any harm or pain I have caused.

I also thank all of the clients who have crossed my path, for allowing me to lead them on their transformational journeys, and for reflecting my beliefs in the human potential to attain unconditional inner peace and resilience.

The outward journey is incomplete without the inward journey. Self-healing is a self-actualization process that involves becoming whole again, starting with addressing the original trauma of separation and disconnection. Not everyone who embarks on this journey reaches the point of experiencing inner peace and remembering the feeling of interconnectedness. Life isn't something to be studied, but rather to be lived. As we do so, we gain a deeper understanding of ourselves and the human experience. It isn't about having all the right answers, but rather, having the capacity to live with the essential questions that life presents to us. By living with these questions, we become the very answers we seek.

Looking back, I never imagined that I would live to see this day...and the creation of this book is beyond my wildest dreams.

For this reason, I owe myself the most love and gratitude for enduring the confusion, hardships, and conflicts that life has presented to me. I am thankful to my younger self for taking a chance at possibilities instead of retreating into my comfort zone. I am grateful for my unyielding will that created miraculous healing within my body, mind, and spirit. And I am thankful for my generous heart, which dedicated long hours of healing creativity to present this book offering to the world.

Work with Chiron

If you're ready to transform subconscious, limiting beliefs and self-sabotaging behaviors, remember the power within, and thrive with radiant health and unconditional happiness, consider partnering with Chiron in one of the following ways.

ONE-ON-ONE COACHING

It takes courage to look within and perform the deep, transformational work that is needed. Self-help books can only take you so far. As an experienced guide, Chiron's personalized care will help you radically love who you are authentically and help you manifest your heart's greatest desires, without the need to fix yourself and the constant strive for perfection.

LIVE EVENTS

Instead of earning another certification, Chiron would love to save you time, energy, and misery in your soul-searching by hosting you at one of his live events. If you are ready to experience full permission to live your life fully and celebrate it with others who are on the same journey, his live events are for you.

ONLINE LIFELINE HEALING CIRCLE

The LifeLine Healing Circle with Chiron integrates the LifeLine Technique® and evolutionary astrology. This support system's focus is to empower you to remember why you are here, discover the higher meaning in your life opportunities and crises, and give you insights on how to align your current path with the universe. By engaging in biweekly gatherings, the potential for enhanced healing outcomes is greatly magnified.

GUEST SPEAKING

Insights have the potential to change our entire life trajectory. More than just sharing information, Chiron's talks, keynotes, and workshops touch the heart of people's lives.

HE IS READY TO SERVE YOU THROUGH THE FOLLOWING TOPICS:

- Astrology
- Holistic healing
- Nature connectedness
- Heart-centered leadership
- The subconscious mind

- Hero's journey
- Life purpose
- Mental health and depression
- Highly sensitive people

Reach out to him with all inquiries at
www.ChironYeng.com.

38102636R00187